Care of Leadership

'Mind works with logic and soul works on ethics; a great leader understands this truth, then he becomes a statesman.'

Shashi Bhushan Dubey, CEO, Sage Consultancy Services, New Dehli, India

'The pace of organisational life today can cause leaders to focus on action at the expense of reflection. While this may be functional in the short term, longer-term performance and learning is optimised when action and reflection interact in a way that each informs the other.

Care of Leadership: A Practice for Developing Leadership Effectiveness weaves theory and best practice in a unique way to offer a pragmatic guided process on how to reflect on leadership practice. The leader who follows this process will gain actionable insights for improved learning and performance, as well as improved personal satisfaction in the leadership role.

I recommend this book to leaders who have the courage to ask deep questions of themselves, to seek constructive feedback from colleagues and to follow through on what emerges in a deeply personal, proactive and self-directed approach to their own development.'

Dr Therese Brady, Organisation Development Consultant

'This book is an engaging and informative way of looking at leadership development. It holds some key techniques and exercises for us to explore ourselves as leaders and our place in the way that leadership is communicated in groups, organisations and society. A great grounding in the leadership learning process.'

Dr Gareth Edwards, Associate Professor of Leadership Development, Bristol Business School

'This outstanding book represents a paradigm shift in leadership thinking. It transitions us from detailing how the core skills, attributes and behaviours of a leader start with self-awareness and mindfulness, which is then used to influence others. It then progresses in a systematic way towards more visible and tangible aspects of leadership which include vision, responsibility, accountability and outcomes. The central theme is that being a leader is a choice and the whole leadership journey is a set of mini-choices. Therefore, the leader has control over every aspect of the journey. However, this book goes much further; it provides a detailed analytical and diagnostic toolkit to enable the leader to deliver outstanding results, in a value-centred and ethical fashion, and helps navigate all the choices that have to be made.'

John J. Barron, Managing Director Reagecon Diagnostics Ltd.

'At its core *Care of Leadership* represents a fervent call to explore our individual leadership potential in order to enhance our personal and professional effectiveness and satisfaction. A composite blend of the academic and the practical, this guide calls attention to what Ann McGarry considers the core building blocks of effective leadership development. Following an account of each of these elements rooted in extant knowledge from research and practice, reflective exercises are presented as part of a process of disciplined capacity building. In this way, McGarry invites the reader on a journey of discovery, the ultimate purpose of which is the development of a true authentic leadership style capable of sustaining us throughout our careers.'

Professor Michael Morley, Kemmy Business School,
University of Limerick

CARE OF LEADERSHIP

A Practice for Developing Leadership Effectiveness

Ann McGarry

ORPEN PRESS

Published by
Orpen Press
Upper Floor, Unit K9
Greenogue Business Park
Rathcoole
Co. Dublin
Ireland

email: info@orpenpress.com
www.orpenpress.com

© Ann McGarry, 2017

Paperback ISBN 978-1-78605-023-6
ePub ISBN 978-1-78605-029-8
Kindle ISBN 978-1-78605-030-4
PDF ISBN 978-1-78605-031-1

Printed in Dublin by SPRINTprint Ltd

To Joe

ABOUT THE AUTHOR

Ann McGarry is a human development consultant who works internationally supporting organisations, teams and individuals to develop and grow. Her coaching and training programmes change peoples' lives and businesses, acting as a catalyst to unleash talent, thereby supporting personal fulfilment whilst also delivering organisational goals.

Her training programmes include leadership, change and strategic management, management development, and wellness, and have been delivered to the public and private sectors, from SMEs to large corporations, either as open or in-house courses. Her highly interactive programmes are content-rich and delivered in a nurturing learning environment.

Ann McGarry, trading as McGarry Consulting, provides quality consultancy services to the highly regulated pharmaceutical and medical devices sectors. Prior to setting up her consultancy practice she held senior quality assurance roles in the pharmaceutical and healthcare sectors for twenty years and staff development formed a significant part of her role.

Her lecturing experience includes the University of Limerick, NUI Galway, Galway–Mayo Institute of Technology and the European Business Institute, delivering on human resource development, supervisory management, quality management and wellness topics.

Ann is a strong advocate of lifelong learning. She graduated with a BSc in Chemistry from NUI Galway in 1977 and also has additional technical qualifications from Dublin Institute of Technology and the Irish Management Institute. Her studies in personal development include a Certificate in Stress Reduction and Relaxation Counselling (Stress Management Institute of Ireland), Diploma in Training and Development (Irish Institute of Training and Development), Certificate in Neuro-Linguistic Programming (Society of NLP) and Diploma in Professional

Coaching (Irish Coach Institute). In 2012 she graduated with an MSc in Work and Organisational Behaviour from University of Limerick.

Her passion for the development of human potential and capacities has inspired her in writing *Care of Leadership.*

Foreword

Care of Leadership presents an exciting and captivating approach to leadership, a subject dear of heart to every business person.

Care of Leadership passionately argues that leadership can be taught. The central theme, the social context of leadership, the essence of the interaction between leaders and followers, is continuously examined. A novel approach based on the mnemonic 'CARE' is adopted.

CA = Conscious Awareness and RE = Reflective Exercises

This book challenges the reader to become consciously aware and to take ownership of their actions and interactions in their leadership role. Reflective exercises presented at the end of each chapter are carefully crafted and present the reader with a choice to take action.

Mind works with logic and soul works on ethics; a great leader understands this truth, then he becomes a statesman. Success and failure comes in everybody's life; a great leader always cares and protects image through intellectual honesty.

From my extensive experience with my IT business enterprises and as a spiritual and life coach I believe that *Care of Leadership* is a tour de force. In my view this book will become essential reading for all leaders.

Ann McGarry has done great work in helping leaders understand how to fill the gap between thinking and being, and this book will help normal leaders to become statesmen.

Shashi Bhushan Dubey
Chief Executive Officer
Sage Consultancy Services
info.sageconsultancyservices@gmail.com
New Delhi, India
3 March 2017

Preface

The business world today is fast-paced, placing high demands on leaders to be effective and flexible, and to change to meet the varied pressures required to survive and thrive. Increasingly, metrics are becoming the new mantras with leaders at all levels in organisations being required to consistently deliver performance to meet the organisations' goals.

More than ever leaders must not only take responsibility for the technical content of their role but must also lead their teams to peak performance to meet and excel in goal achievement. Leaders need to strike a balance between creating a stimulating and motivating environment for individuals and teams alike to develop and grow, and also fulfilling their organisations' goals. When organisations face challenging times and fail to achieve expected targets it is the systems which come under focus and oftentimes little or inadequate attention is given to the leadership dimension. While training and development of leaders remains a putative high priority for organisations it may still remain a human resource management challenge.

It was with this backdrop that the valuable insights gained in my own career and my consultancy practice led me to write *Care of Leadership*. I must also admit my passion for personal development and my unceasing interest in observing people and leaders in action was also a factor. Yet another motivation stems from my desire to move from the more traditional approaches still seen in the content of many training courses offered in the marketplace. I wanted to create a programme that deals with the heart of the issue: the social context of leadership. My desire is to ensure that this book and its supporting programmes have practical application, not confined to the narrower focus of skill development but rather the focus is directed at the slower development of core leadership qualities.

Care of Leadership presents the reassuring message that leadership can be taught. Through these pages I hope that you will view the approach taken as refreshing. The book invites you, the leaders, to take charge of your own development.

Care of Leadership places a particular emphasis on the social context of leadership. This is the exchange between leader and follower which underscores the importance of having a good match between both parties and the images that they hold on what constitutes a good leader.

Care of Leadership has been written as a practice, using a coaching approach. The combined skills of conscious awareness and reflective practice are invoked at the end of each of the ten chapters, which discuss the identified core qualities for leadership development. A call for a commitment to take action follows. This approach provides the necessary stimulus for the reader to actively engage with the material presented and not just be a passive reader. In doing so it supports practical leadership development and thereby moves beyond more traditional approaches adopted on this subject.

Care of Leadership is a slim book with high impact, providing a provocative treatment of the essential qualities in the development of leadership effectiveness embracing the whole leader. It cuts to the chase, supporting leaders to bring forth the best they can be.

For me, *Care of Leadership* has been a labour of love, tapping into my overarching goal in life to grow and evolve and in so doing to support others in their awakening to fully realising their potential.

I hope that you enjoy the next steps on your leadership journey.

Ann McGarry
Galway
24 February 2017

Acknowledgments

In bringing *Care of Leadership* from manuscript to publication it is important to recognise the significant contributions of:

Gerry O'Connor, Orpen Press, who heard my passion for *Care of Leadership* and believed in its potential influence for business leaders.

Eileen O'Brien, my editor, for her invaluable support and advice throughout the editing process and her caring for this novice author.

Joe Coughlan, my husband, for his love, support and encouragement in getting *Care of Leadership* over the line.

And finally to my parents, James (deceased) and Sarah, for the gift of education and love of learning.

CONTENTS

Part I

Introduction

An Academic Perspective on Leadership

Leadership is arguably the most widely researched topic in both psychology and business today. Improving leadership development was identified as the most important human resource priority for organisations in a survey of 5,561 executives spread over 109 countries (Strack et al., 2010 cited in DeRue, Sitkin and Podolny, 2011, p. 369). IBM's Global Business Services (2008) survey on human capital issues identifies the lack of leadership capability as one of the top workforce challenges, with 75 per cent of companies indicating that building leadership talent is a significant challenge (Day, Harrison and Halpin, 2009). When one considers the commitment of organisations to leadership development these figures, at best, are worrying. In the US, 25 per cent of organisations' annual spend ($50 billion) on learning and development is targeted at leadership development (O'Leonard, 2010, cited in DeRue et al., 2011, p. 369). Day (2001, p. 581) stated that 'the interest in leadership development seems to be at its zenith', while Schyns, Kiefer, Kerschreiter and Tymon (2011, p. 397) stated 'yet a decade later interest in leader and leadership development seems to be unbroken in academia and, of course, in practice.'

The focus of academic literature has mainly been placed on leaders – their related skills, characteristics and behaviours – with training and development mirroring this traditional approach. Consequently, the social context (leadership development) receives noticeably less attention in research and practice than that of the individual leaders (leader development). Although there have been advances in examining the social context of leadership development in recent years, including Implicit Leadership Theories (ILTs) – the everyday images that everyone holds about leaders – this is still an area that deserves further attention. ILTs emphasise the role of the perceptual process and highlight

3

the importance of the social context – the leadership process. Teaching ILTs develops leaders and leadership, raising awareness of both the social context and one's own ILTs and the match or otherwise between both – the essence of understanding leader–follower interactions and leading to the process of claiming and granting leader identity.

It is in the social context of the leader–follower exchange that leadership development can be enhanced. This is the environment where a leader, on the one hand, sees and identifies him/herself as a leader in the performance of his/her role, and, on the other hand, his/her direct reports (the followers) deem this leader to be a leader. In this claiming and granting process, the social leader–follower exchange is crucial to the leadership role. This book encourages leaders to step back and view their interactions. Through the reflective questioning process leaders can both increase their self-awareness and enhance their social awareness and thereby increase their effectiveness in the leadership process.

In my MSc thesis, 'Implicit Leadership Theories and Leadership Development' (McGarry, 2012), I examined leadership development through a training intervention using an ILT drawing exercise to determine whether leader identity can be enhanced through this process. Building on the work of Schyns et al. (2011), I applied a composite scale for leader and leadership development with measurement both pre- and post the ILT intervention (McGarry, 2012). The thesis also included a brief questionnaire to study subjects' intentions and actual follow-up. This study attempted to include the work environment context in the exploration of ILTs in leadership development. Four main themes emerged from the research findings, but the twin themes of leader identity and ability to learn from experience are more significant from an individual leader standpoint as these remain under the direct control of the individual leader. The third theme is availability of feedback (support), which may be viewed as an external influence. The final theme, shift in leader identity, may be seen as the output of the combination of the first three themes. Shift in leader identity ultimately is the most significant as this reflects the effectiveness of the process. 'Implicit Leadership Theories and Leadership Development' (McGarry, 2012) may be considered the foundational study to this book, *Care of Leadership*.

A Personal Note: How This Book Came to Be

In 2005 I had a desire to write a book, one which would be worthy of some merit and that in a small way would be of benefit to the business community. The concept of the book would be on leadership from a personal perspective. At that time I had already started my own personal journey attending personal development seminars and training in an effort to find myself and bring forth the best possible version of me. This period was marked by writing a dozen or so vignettes. In addition, I struggled with attempts to make an impression on the personal development subject matter. A few pages on three topics were the meagre results for this effort but no book material in sight.

At a motivational and self-improvement event, 'Mega' Seminar Series with Mark Victor Hansen in Los Angeles in 2008, I rubbed shoulders with a number of the personal development celebrity presenters. I had hoped that my attendance at this seminar would provide me with a kickstart into the personal development consultancy aspect of my business. I followed up with Carolyn McCormick's Business Bootcamp for Speakers, Authors and Coaches in Denver a couple of months later. There were a number of projects which I had in mind to bring to the public arena, some of which have been delivered. However, the idea of writing a book on personal leadership which could apply to both those with formal positions of authority and leaders without a title had not quite taken shape and was nowhere near book format.

The completion of my MSc in Work and Organisational Behaviour in 2012 and my research thesis on leadership development was the fitting framework on which to hang the ideas and the chapters which had been percolating in my head over the previous years. With the dawning that this book had a contextual framework in 2014 I stated my intent to write a book to support leadership development. Over my managerial career, I had felt that leadership programmes in the main had missed the point and solely focused on the leader's traits, characteristics, behaviour and skills. Having had a keen interest in personal development and spirituality for over twenty years I felt that most of the programmes were lacking in this dimension, that this area was viewed as too fluffy and not having a place in the hard world of business. For the first time since the initial rumblings of the book I now had clarity of purpose and really a greater core belief in myself that I was now aligned with my purpose.

This book has had a long gestation period punctuated with a number of starts and stops, with my quality consultancy projects pulling me away from the discipline of writing and focusing my efforts for this book. In hindsight it is only since 2015 that this book stood any chance of being written. The previous year, although marked with the dawning of the book context, I had busied myself with much work on quality consultancy projects outside of Ireland. Devoid of space there was no real room for this creative project. Also on a deeper personal level, I needed to fill myself with confidence in putting myself out there and joy that my dream was finally coming to fruition.

I am writing this book to pass on my knowledge and insights to a future generation of leaders. My dear hope is that you the reader will find this book good enough to encourage you to reflect on your role as a leader and make whatever changes are required for you to grow and develop into the best leader you can be.

'There is nothing so powerful as an idea whose time has come.'

Victor Hugo

And finally, my 'WHY'.

My overarching goal in life is to develop my talents and gifts and utilise these to the fullest extent possible. On this journey my desire is to support others in the pursuit and realisation of their goals, either at an individual or organisational level. This journey, which started in 1993, continues, developing many facets, while deepening my understanding and knowing of me.

'We shall not cease from exploration and the end of all our exploring will be to arrive where we started and know the place for the first time.'

T.S. Eliot

Conscious Awareness and Reflective Exercise(s)

Conscious Awareness

Being consciously aware means being 'tuned into' life. Central to this process is that you become more aware of yourself – your thoughts, actions and behaviours. As you become more conscious the effects of your thoughts and actions come into sharp focus. With this awareness comes freedom of choice – you are free to choose how to act and behave. As conscious awareness develops further you have the opportunity to choose greater degrees of self-regulating behaviour. With such a dawning, a knowing develops that there are causes and consequences to the actions you choose to take.

Our actions and behaviours are governed by the way we feel, with emotions playing a central role. So emotions are our greatest barometer to our well-being. How we feel has a powerful impact on our lives. We all have experience of feeling upbeat and positive while in other instances we have all also experienced being in low spirits and down in the doldrums. We can change the way we feel by thinking different thoughts. This also means that we don't have to be a prisoner to our feelings. We have the power to change the way we feel, act and behave. We have the power to act to change the situation. For example, think of working with someone who constantly nags us or puts us down. Instead of feeling depressed and hopeless about the situation we can choose to confront this person and indeed remove ourself from this environment altogether. So instead of playing the victim role we can move to take action and regain control of our life and take responsibility for the life we wish to create.

Conscious awareness heightens the notion that we are powerful and that we can create the life we want.

Reflective Exercise(s), i.e. Reflective Practices

Reflection is thinking about what you do. It is an integral part of learning. The learning cycle, according to Kolb (1984), is a four-step process: concrete experience, reflective observation, abstract conceptualisation and active experimentation. Much of Kolb's theory is concerned with the learner's internal cognitive processes. Kolb (1984) states that learning involves the acquisition of abstract concepts that can be applied flexibly in a range of situations.

In Kolb's theory, the impetus for the development of new concepts is provided by new experiences. 'Learning is the process whereby knowledge is created through the transformation of experience' (Kolb, 1984, p. 38).

Reflection, which involves conscious effort, is the mechanism by which you review the situation and develop insights. From this point comes the notion of what you might do differently the next time. Chris Argyris (1999), who coined the term 'double loop learning', explains the idea of reflection as that of stepping out of the single loop of experience, reflection, conceptualisation and application and entering into a second loop to recognise a new paradigm and reframe your ideas in order to change what you do.

Reflective practice is a skill which can be learned. It has been described as an active, dynamic, action-based and ethical set of skills, placed in real time and dealing with real, complex and difficult situations.

There are six fundamental stages of reflective processes:

- Stage 1: Selecting a critical incident to reflect upon
- Stage 2: Observing and describing that experience
- Stage 3: Analysing that experience
- Stage 4: Interpreting that experience
- Stage 5: Exploring alternatives
- Stage 6: Framing action

The rewards from engaging in reflective practices are many, not least those of emotional intelligence and integrity.

Self-awareness, one of the four dimensions to emotional intelligence, can be increased through reflective practice. Self-awareness provides a handle to view your thoughts, emotions, actions and behaviours. This in turn can have a potential knock-on effect on two other emotional intelligence dimensions – those of self-management and social awareness. The effect of your actions on yourself as well as on others can be observed. This may then result in taking action and perhaps change, thereby affecting the self-management dimension. As the dynamic of these three aspects of emotional intelligence change they in turn affect the fourth dimension: relationship management.

Integrity is affected and enhanced through the reflective process when you touch your core values. Through reflection you are given the opportunity to establish whether you are in tune or otherwise with your values and then take appropriate steps for correction as needed to restore harmony.

A simple and practical way to apply reflective practices is by keeping a personal journal and taking a few minutes at the end of each day to reflect on your activities and interactions. A further opportunity for reflection is prompted by the reflective exercises (RE) within each of the chapters on 'LEADERSHIP'.

So to sum up, conscious awareness (CA) coupled with reflective exercise(s) (RE) form the basis of CARE of Leadership.

Care of Leadership and **How to Use this Book**

Care of Leadership is a practical guide, a practice to leadership development. Ten topics are introduced which focus on core qualities of the word 'LEADERSHIP'. Each of these topics is then expanded through 'CARE', getting you actively involved in your own development through conscious awareness (CA) and reflective exercises (RE). CA-RE is the essential stimulus for leadership development, the prompt for you, the leader, to your responsibility, to take action to develop and grow in the social context of leadership – the leader–follower exchange. Awareness is the key which precedes any actions in behavioural change. Firstly, the trigger event or stimulus must first be seen. Secondly, your reaction to this event must be viewed and this includes both your thoughts and actions. As with any change process it must be accompanied by the desire and willingness for change. Each chapter concludes with a prompt to take action and set goals which can be integrated into your daily work.

There are a number of techniques referenced in the Appendix which you may find helpful in engaging with the material within this book. Activities include journaling, visualisation, affirmation, meditation, goal-setting and the benefits of reflection.

The ten chapters examine the following topics (with their respective sub-topics): purpose (and power and performance); identity (and influence and integrity); hope (and humour); seeking out (and self-esteem); responsibility (and results); emotional intelligence (with its four elements of self-awareness, self-management, social aware-ness and relationship management); development (and delegation); accountability (and achievement and acknowledgement); energy of emergence (and ego and essence); and leading (and listening, looking and learning). This chapter sequence appears in reverse order to the spelling of LEADERSHIP. In so doing we start with the end in mind – 'Purpose' – and close with the last chapter on 'Leading'. Subtopics included within each chapter have direct relevance to the main topic of a given chapter.

Each chapter begins with a brief discussion of an aspect of leader-ship, which is followed by a series of reflective questions designed to prompt you not only to view your own actions as a leader but also to reflect on the impact of your interactions on others and your fol-lowers. Through engagement in answering these reflective questions and active participation with this process you will get useful insights. Change and action may be required as you journey deeper into more effective levels of leadership. In the concluding section of each chapter, 'Commitment to Take Action', it is hoped that you embrace this prompt to maximise your potential to learn, develop and grow. Integrating these actions into the routine goals and objectives will develop you as a leader.

I recommend that you start in the order that the book is laid out. Devote up to one month to each chapter, reading through it initially at the start of the first week. Closely observe yourself over the month. Pay particular attention to your interactions with your team and the wider organisation. At the close of the month carve out some 'me' time using the questions developed for the chapter to prompt reflection as you journal. Following this I would suggest committing to a maximum of three actions which you intend to work on over the coming months. These could be arranged as goals and if possible using the 'SMART' format (i.e. specific, measurable, attainable (and action-focused), real-istic (and relevant), and time-bound). I recommend that you would incorporate these actions into your diary and track them through to completion. On a quarterly basis I suggest you review and reflect on your progress and commit to your continuous development.

Care of Leadership is intended for leaders in all types of business from both public and private sectors: commercial, financial, industrial and academic. It lends itself equally well to small businesses and to multinationals. At an individual level its relevance extends beyond individual leaders in a formal role to those who are leaders with no formal powers.

It is also hoped that this book finds relevance in the academic world and possible use as a teaching aid on formal managerial programmes and studies.

I wish you bon voyage on the discovery and the development of this highest aspect of you in your leadership role.

To conclude, I would be deeply interested in hearing from you with your stories on know how this book has helped and supported your journey in leadership development. Please refer to page 150 for our contact details.

Part II

Introduction

The essence of leadership is introduced over the next ten chapters. Chapter 1 opens with *purpose*, inviting you to examine purpose. What is the purpose of your life? What is your purpose as a leader and also that of your organisation? This chapter encourages you to check on the resonance between the broader picture and your role within your organisation. Leadership, from the standpoint of the leader's *identity*, is discussed in Chapter 2. In this second chapter you are asked to reflect on your identity as a leader, firstly in the context of self and secondly as it relates to your followers. This chapter focuses on possibly one of the most significant dimensions of leadership: bringing the leader's image of leadership into sharp focus and clearly forming a direct linkage with the introductory chapter, purpose. *Hope*, the topic of Chapter 3, looks at your attitude towards and outlook on life and the mind-set that you, as a leader, bring to your role. *Seeking out*, as it relates to feedback and opportunities to learn, is introduced in Chapter 4 as a pathway to develop potentials and it is combined with the subject of self-esteem. *Responsibility*, the theme presented in Chapter 5, links into the aspect of having choice in how you react to any given situation. The crucial element of successful leadership, *emotional intelligence*, is the subject of Chapter 6. *Development* is the subject matter for Chapter 7 and is linked with delegation. Chapter 8 addresses the subject matter of *accountability* and a number of allied themes: achievement of aims (goals) and the acknowledgement and appreciation of actions. This chapter stresses the importance of the leader having ultimate accountability for the success or otherwise of the area's goals. In addition, emphasis is placed on fully recognising the important role your followers play in departmental/area success. *Energy of emergence*, the subject of Chapter 9, introduces your energy and the importance of going within to tap into your essence. The final chapter looks at *leading* and being comfortable with and loving your leadership role. It also examines the importance of listening both within and from the outside for clues as to your effectiveness as a leader. So now let us begin.

1

PURPOSE

POWER AND PERFORMANCE

'The purpose of life is not to be happy. It is to be useful, to be honorable, to be compassionate, to have it make some difference that you have lived and lived well.'

Ralph Waldo Emerson

Introduction

This opening chapter introduces the question of purpose. As leaders it is important to examine what does purpose mean to you not only for yourself in your life as a whole but also in the context that you have been placed in a position of power in your role as leader. Power and performance, as related themes to purpose, are also discussed in this chapter.

Purpose

Purpose essentially is about 'finding meaning'. It concerns itself with the wider focus of your whole and entire life. Included within this is the narrower aspect, possibly a more familiar focus, of your work life. Finding meaning, finding purpose within your life and your working life is important and you choose the activities and interactions which follow as a result. But are you consciously aware that these are choices? Or would you rather believe that they automatically flow from your working life? There is an outflow from you to all your relationships and connections. Knowing and connecting with your purpose and the meaning you associate with this informs your interactions in your relationships with the people who are close to you: your family, friends, colleagues and team members. Purpose and your conscious activities affect all the different roles you play in your life; purpose affects your beliefs, attitudes and actions.

What motivates you in living your life can be viewed as comprising four main elements with your entire human being stemming from them. These elements span the dimensions of physical, mental, emotional/social and spiritual (Covey et al., 1994). According to the motivational theory by Maslow (1943) known as the Hierarchy of Needs, human needs progress from one level to the next once satisfied. In ascending order, the lower level needs are physiological, safety and security, and belonging. These three needs are referred to as 'dependency' needs. The two further needs of esteem and self-actualisation are higher order and are termed 'growth' needs. Self-actualisation, at its deepest level, taps into finding purpose and meaning, and living from this space of knowing and expressing it to the full potential. In essence it is living, breathing and actively engaging in the development of all your potentials – your unique gifts and talents.

Returning to the four aspects of your physical, mental, emotional/social and spiritual needs, you need to take care of, and attend to, each of these aspects to ensure that they are balanced. Giving more focus to one over another or indeed ignoring one at the expense of another will not end with a desirable outcome long-term. For a truly happy life these four aspects need not only to be integrated but synergies should be sought between them rather than just developing each one in isolation (Covey et al., 1994). Ultimately, all the needs grow to support one overarching aim: finding purpose in life.

Finding your true purpose can be a life-long quest, a mission that may not always be realised, and in fact the quest, the journey itself, may become your purpose. Travelling this journey consciously, living each moment consciously, may be the purpose. In the deepest meaning, purpose is the journey home to your true Self – the part within you that is true love, all perfect, divine. Getting in touch with your true Self, this inner state, is a gradual process which takes time and patience. The more this inner state is tapped into the more you live without fear.

Living from this state of being is living an ordinary everyday of life from an extraordinary place, a place of inner knowing, and a place of bliss.

Knowledge about this way of living is one thing; however, living in this state of Being is truly powerful. Now, with confidence all that is necessary is to set the goal, keeping your intention on the goal, and knowing with certainty that the goal will be realised, while engaging in activities consciously in every moment.

So, your journey into leadership development opens with the big question on purpose – 'What is your (life's) purpose?', and also, 'What is your role, your purpose, as a leader?' It may appear daunting at first. For some it may even be off-putting. I encourage you to stay with it. Let's look at it another way. Is it not true that you would ask such a question at the outset of any work project? The reality is most probably that you would not even query the relevance of the question as you would believe it to be both logical and necessary to have clarity at the outset.

Life's 'purpose' or 'vision' is a primary motivation of human action. It is the ability to see beyond your present reality and to create and become what you are not yet. As mentioned previously, life's purpose can be a journey rather than a destination, with the steps along the way of equal importance to the actual destination. Life's purpose or vision, with its associated passion, can be incredibly powerful. It can fuel and sustain you to surmount even the most difficult of obstacles. It can become so engrained in you that it becomes the compelling force behind your every decision.

Delving deeply into your life demands a degree of soul-searching and questioning of your life, choices and actions taken.

'The unexamined life is not worth living.'

Socrates

Taking a somewhat narrower focus, purpose can be explored through the lens of your role as a leader in your organisation. It may be beneficial to make the distinction between a leader and a manager: the main difference is that leaders have people who follow them while managers have people who work for them. An individual in a managerial position needs to be both a leader and a manager. Leadership is about creating a vision, which is both compelling and passionately held by the leader, and then communicating it clearly to one's followers, who buy into that vision and work confidently and effectively towards the achievement of the desired goals. Managing is mainly focused on administering and making sure the day-to-day activities are happening as intended. While there are many ways of viewing leaders – such as examining their traits and characteristics, or their situational behavioural approach – the crucial understanding of the social context of leadership and its application far outweighs these other methods.

As a leader you need to lead consciously from the social context of leadership environment and engage the following:

- *Vision* – knowing where you are and where you want to go to, and getting buy-in from your followers
- *Communication skills* – essential for your vision, for providing regular updates on progress, including issues you face along the journey, for the free flow of ideas, and as a vehicle of two-way communication upwards and downwards
- *Inspiration* – ensuring that your team understand their role in the bigger picture and play to their highest potential
- *Honesty and integrity* – crucial for getting buy-in from the team to commit to your vision
- *Challenge* – be an independent thinker and be sufficiently brave to do things differently if needed

Managing is about taking the vision and making it a reality through devising a plan with the necessary steps to be followed. It is also about directing the day-to-day activities, reviewing the resources needed and anticipating needs along the way. Process management is yet another aspect, involving designing processes, performance standards and operational procedures. Finally, it is also people-focused, with respect to managing their needs and gaining their commitment to work completion.

At the heart of leadership development is an understanding that it takes place in a social context and, to be effective as a leader, firstly, you must be willing to take on the role of 'leader', not just manager and, secondly, your team, or followers, must individually recognise that you are a leader and grant you the authority to lead, not just manage. This topic will be further developed in Chapter 2.

Power

Integral to your position as a leader is the aspect of power. There is a power differential between you and your team. You are the leader but have you considered how you are using this power difference? Have you consciously given this any consideration? The critical question to ask is 'how do you use this power?' Do you choose to avoid recognition of your power, preferring to have everyone on buddy-buddy relationship terms, favouring harmony over potential confrontation and never rocking the boat? Or do you simply over-use your power? In Chapter 2 this will be discussed in more detail.

Performance

Crucial to the ongoing success of any business is the measurement of performance. The business of leading your team is no different. In today's business environment key performance indicators (KPIs) are the standard mode of measurement but can you really talk about communication, coaching, encouraging, relationship-building and team process in terms of efficiency? Surely effectiveness is the measure that is needed. Furthermore, the time scales in relation to these aspects may not be effectively measured on the tight time scales demanded by the traditional use of KPIs.

As a leader your performance should be measured in terms of how you lead. Integral to this is developing your staff and a key characteristic of effective leadership is surrounding yourself with a strong team. This requires you to effectively delegate so that you develop your team, and both encourage and support them to be the best they can be. Achieving this requires a time investment in each member of your team. Besides setting goals and objectives for team members, monitoring their progress is essential. Time invested in coaching is well spent in supporting members of your team to effectively achieve their goals. Ultimately, this ensures the successful outcome for the unit's objectives.

By acting in inclusive ways when setting goals – feeling and enjoying the satisfaction of shared achievements by you, the leader, and your team – the act of valuing the contributions of all members provides the ingredients for more successful outcomes for future projects. Recognising the achievement of your followers at various intervals throughout a process is essential. In essence, these are the building blocks for effective working relationships and creating a positive working environment. These topics will be revisited in further chapters.

Finally, before leaving this first chapter I would like to share some concepts in relation to motivation which I recently reconnected with when re-reading *Coaching for Improved Work Performance* by Ferdinand F. Fournies (2000). He states that with Maslow's theory there is an assumption that if managers can identify the follower's dominant need and then identify the elements of work that will satisfy that need the follower will be motivated. In a nutshell, the assumption is that by having long conversations with the follower a manager will know what is going on in that follower's head. Fournies (2000) also references Douglas McGregor (1960), famous for his management approach classification as Theory X versus Theory Y (where X assumes most people find work distasteful, prefer direction, lack ambition and have little desire for responsibility, and Y assumes people are not lazy or unreliable, are capable of self-direction and are creative to meet required goals). According to Fournies (2000), the most important conclusion which can be drawn from this theory is about managers and not workers: that the manager's actions are driven by their beliefs about the workers and managers are not as effective as they should be face-to-face because of their 'unfounded and erroneous (and self-destructive) beliefs about workers' (Fournies, 2000, p. 34).

Herzberg (1966) and his motivational influences describes the 'Satisfiers' as achievement, recognition, work itself and responsibility; and the 'Dissatisfiers' as company policy, administration, supervision, work conditions and salary. It should be stated that the elimination of dissatisfaction does not necessarily provide satisfaction. In relation to achievement and recognition, Fournies (2000, p. 36) claims that managers 'behave contrary to his [Herzberg's] findings; we spend a lot of time convincing people that the good work they produce is normal – that what they achieve is what was expected anyhow, and that's what they get paid for'. The top three reasons gleaned from Fournies' (2000) seminars as to why managers avoid recognition of achievement were identified as:

- They don't have enough time to manage
- They are not aware of the numerous forms of recognition
- They have a warped sense of achievement

Fournies (2000, p. 40) introduces an interesting concept of 'failing by less' as an achievement. Simply put, someone has done something for the first time or has done it better than before. Herzberg said that people are not motivated by failure, they are motivated by achievement. Small achievements act as motivators for someone to go on to try to achieve a little bit more.

THE CARE OF PURPOSE, POWER AND PERFORMANCE

Consider carefully the below questions and statements and then use the space provided to write down your answers.

Purpose (Life)

- Have you ever spent time wondering what the purpose of your life is?
- Do you get a nagging feeling when you reflect on your life?
- Are you doing things that are nurturing and energising you? Are they adding enjoyment to your life?
- Do you have hobbies and aspirations that you have long-fingered and dismissed as mere pipe dreams?
- Have you settled for less? Why?
- Are you sapped of energy and feel that you are merely 'existing' rather that feeling fully alive?
- In Maslow's hierarchy of needs the lower needs must be achieved before moving on to the higher order needs. The movement through to the higher needs is seen as your life's journey. Where do you see yourself right now? Are you satisfied with where you are now? What feelings arise for you?

_____
_____
_____
_____
_____
_____
_____
_____
_____
_____
_____
_____
_____

The aspects of your life can be depicted in the following terms:

- *Physical*: your physical body – fitness, health, nutrition; and money – potential to earn your living

- *Mental*: mental health – anxiety, regular worrying thoughts, view of life through a negative filter; and mental stimulation – being educated sufficiently, being engaged by your work, enjoying the process of work knowing that you are making a significant contribution to the overall goals
- *Emotional/social*: family relationships, friends and significant other
- *Spiritual*: engagement in spiritual practice on a regular basis; developing spiritually by reading uplifting books; connecting inwards each day; spending time in nature and spending time alone in reflection

For each of the above areas write down any thoughts they inspire.

How would you describe the level of importance you give each of these areas in your life? Are they balanced? Could you find ways of improving and integrating these in a synergistic way rather than working on each in isolation?

As you develop all these aspects of your life, know that you are developing holistically. You are easily and effortlessly spending time developing yourself and growing in all your roles in life.

How does the above statement affect you? Your roles can be many, e.g. husband/wife/partner, sister/brother, daughter/son, career role, community/hobbies/interests.

_____
_____
_____
_____
_____
_____
_____
_____
_____
_____
_____

- What changes could you make to feel more fulfilled, more alive?
- What additions could you make?
- What is preventing you from taking action?
- What are you willing to do to make your life happier?
- What goals can you set right now?

Purpose (Work): Your Role as a Leader

- How do your personal life purpose and goals align with the organisation you are working for?
- Have you truly developed all your capacities within your role as leader? Where have you excelled? Where have you fallen short? What are the reasons? What actions can you take?
- Have you embodied the qualities of a leader? Do you consistently demonstrate these? Do you lead by example?
- In relation to staff have you spent time with each person and developed their roles? Have you explained to them how they fit in and what their contribution means to the unit/department and the organisation as a whole so that they understand their purpose?
- Have you developed your staff to their full potential within their roles? Have you created opportunities for them to develop?
- Consider the following statement in relation to how you actually lead your team: 'leaders do what they do to their followers because of what they believe about their followers.'
- When was the last time you recognised the achievements of each member of your team other than at the formal performance appraisal process? For example:

  - Thank you
  - That was a very good job
  - I appreciate the effort which you put into that

- You are really progressing; with 97 per cent of your work being error-free this is very promising.

_____
_____
_____
_____
_____
_____
_____
_____
_____
_____
_____
_____

Power and Performance: Your Role as a Leader

- How have you approached your role of leading others? Have you led using an encouraging approach? Or have you led using your position of power to ensure that work activities are achieved?
- Are you delegating effectively? Have you identified projects that are challenging to develop staff and help them reach their potential?
- Do you believe that investing time in coaching your followers to make their contribution count is an important goal – your true goal as a leader? Do you see this as one of your strengths or as something that diminishes your power?
- How do you use the performance management tool? Would you describe your use of the tool as effective or are you just going through the motions, completing it in a rushed and hurried way just to ensure that you have fulfilled this requirement?
- Have you reviewed your followers' performance in an objective and consistent way? Have you based your reviews on the facts? Have the facts been gathered over a period of time or are they a reflection of isolated incidents?
- Have you been prompt in your feedback when it was required?
- How successful do you think you are in face-to-face discussions with your followers? What if you were told now that your beliefs about your followers are unfounded and erroneous? Would you act

differently if you believed all your followers wanted to and indeed were capable of being successful?

_____

_____

_____

_____

_____

_____

_____

_____

_____

_____

_____

_____

COMMITMENT TO TAKE ACTION

Before completing this final section take the time to review what you have written up to now. Then create a space, some quiet time, for you to really connect with yourself and see what you truly want to commit to.

For this process stay out of your head as much as possible and instead connect with your heart. Ask of it what is best for you at this time to commit to. When you are ready, take up to three actions to work on over the coming months.

Set these as goals in SMART format, ensuring that you are including specific details on the actions necessary. You also will need to measure your progress so decide on the measurement and the frequency for each undertaking. Then transfer these actions and goals to your regular working documents, e.g. your diary.

Finally, before leaving this chapter please sign and date your commitment to these actions below.

Chapter 1 – Purpose: Goal 1

_____

_____

_____

_____

_____

Chapter 1 – Purpose: Goal 2

_____

_____

_____

_____

_____

Chapter 1 – Purpose: Goal 3

_____

_____

_____

_____

_____

Sign and Date

_____   _____

IDENTITY (LEADER IDENTITY)

INFLUENCE AND INTEGRITY

'First say to yourself what you would be; then do what you have to do.'

Epictetus

Introduction

Leader identity – how you perceive yourself – is the crucial element of effective leadership. In this chapter leader identity is discussed, firstly, in terms of the development of identity and, following this, four domains influencing identity, related to a leader's beliefs and perceptions, are introduced. Influence and integrity, as important ingredients in leadership, are also discussed as being integral to the leader being recognised and accepted by the team.

Identity: Leader Identity

Identity relates to how you perceive yourself in relation to the environment, including relationships with others and assimilation into societal norms, beliefs and standards (Bronfenbrenner, 1979, as cited in Day et al., 2009, p. 57). So leader identity plays a major role in shaping your reactions and contributions to social life. Identity is important because it grounds your understanding of who you are, and what your hopes and goals are, as well as your strengths and challenges. A fully developed and integrated leader identity can be beneficial in building confidence in the key skills of both interpersonal communications and decision-making, particularly when dealing with new and uncertain circumstances (Baumeister, 1995, cited by Day et al., 2009).

Identity Development

Identity development is a complex area that is outside the scope of this book; however, the main aspects in relation to leadership development are discussed below following a review of the key literature.

Identity can comprise sub-identities with the integration of various components of oneself. Self-development and identity development are divided into distinct development (which focuses on development stages) and organisational perspective on predicting work-related outcomes). Marcia's work (1966), as cited by Day et al. (2009), provides a framework on 'crisis' and 'commitment', the former referring to the decision period where the identity options are explored and tried out, while the latter refers to the settling on a component for self-identification. The extensive review of development identity by Bosma and Kunnen (2001) noted three determinants of identity development: (1) openness to experience and change in the individuals; (2) the importance of context in terms of support and opportunities for growth; and (3) the importance of the outcome of previous development. Development is cyclical and an iterative process of conflict and resolution between an individual's commitment and information from the environment. Day et al. (2009) state that healthy development is achieved through a balance between assimilation (i.e. the individual adjusts their interpretation of the context to be consistent with self-schema) and accommodation (the individual adjusts their commitments or identity). Loevinger (1976), as cited by Day et al. (2009), emphasises the role of social cognition, arguing that reasoning and understanding about one's own experiences in terms of the role of self and others shapes identity formation, with eight stages of ego growth increasing in sophistication and responding to environmental demands. Loevinger (1976) identifies three areas of ego growth: impulse control, interpersonal relationships and conscious preoccupations. Experiences upsetting the equilibrium of an existing stage, which are personally notable, emotional and of an interpersonal nature, are thought to facilitate ego stage transition (Manners, Durkin and Nesdale, 2004). An individual's overall identity develops as the sub-identities are expanded, defined and integrated through experience, self-reflection and discourse (Day et al., 2009). Referring to Kegan (1982, 1994), Day et al. (2009) state that development occurs when an individual experiences and deals with increasingly complex situations, and integrates these with the self-awareness that they can experience impulses but are not defined by those impulses.

Social group membership can also develop identity, examining the role of the collective self in group and intergroup processes. Social identity has been defined as 'that part of an individual's self-concept which derives from his/her knowledge of his/her membership of a social group (or groups) together with the value and emotional significance attached to that membership' (Tajfel, 1978, p. 63). Day et al. (2009) argue that changes in identity can be internalised through social validation processes involving feedback from important others in one's work network.

Leadership is the 'most conspicuous manifestation of social effectiveness' and implies that a person's social competence is honed enough to attract a following (Link, 1950, p. 7, as cited by Day et al., 2009).

A developed identity provides a leader with an understanding of their words and actions and how they may be perceived by others. The building of trust can also be enhanced by the adaptation of identity within the context of collaborative intention. Emerging self-awareness is coupled with identity development. Self-awareness is often described as being critical for leader development and success.

The way we perceive ourselves, our self-concept or identity, strongly informs our feelings, beliefs, attitudes, goals and behaviour and directly contributes to the saliency of our identity. Your identity or self-concept is one of the most significant regulators of behaviour (Schlenker, 1980) and self-concept has a broad impact on your life, on shifts in your self-esteem, mood changes, social comparison choices, nature of self-representation, choice of social setting, and the meaning attached to your situation (Markus and Wurf, 1987). Self-concept is dynamic and negotiated through interacting with other people (Goffman, 1959).

To conclude, Muir and Zheng (2012) state that researchers have lamented the narrow focus of leadership development on skill development (Lord and Hall, 2005), stating that they have called for a shifted focus on slower development of core leadership qualities, and for the integration of the leader identity into one's self-schema (Day and Lance, 2004; Lord and Hall, 2005).

Leader Identity: Leadership Beliefs and Leadership Self-Identity

Four domains which impact on leader identity, relating to a leader's beliefs and perceptions, were identified and a questionnaire developed by Hiller (2005), which I applied to my studies on a small group of leaders (McGarry, 2012). These studies found that each of the four domains – leader self-perception and 'relational' perception within a group context (leadership self-identity) and beliefs about dominance and development (leadership beliefs) – had an important impact on these subjects in their leadership roles. Leader self-perception relates to how you see yourself in your role as a leader. The degree to which you associate yourself with your role as a leader has a significant bearing on this aspect of identity – perception. If you are doubtful and uncertain in your role as leader this will negatively impact on your leadership effectiveness. Confidence in your role as leader, on the other hand, will positively impact on leadership effectiveness and will mean you strongly associate with your role as leader. The 'relational' perception is about seeing the leadership role in the context of the team and understanding that the team is the environment in which you function, operate and engage. Simply put, unless there are followers there can be no leader. Therefore, understanding 'relational' perception, the social context of leadership, is vital to effective leadership. Dominance, the third domain, relates to the formal position which you hold as leader and its associated power. There is a power difference between you, as the leader, and your followers. The key here is how you lead and whether this power difference is used wisely and positively. Dominance could be viewed by some leaders as a valid application, using one's position to get the job done. Do you feel all-powerful and rule through fear, leaving your followers little choice but to comply with orders or face the consequences? The fourth domain is that of development and the belief you hold as to whether you can develop into this role of leadership, dispelling the belief that leaders are born. Agreeing with the notion that you can develop into the leadership role is the belief that training and experience are extremely beneficial to any leader, and therefore by identifying with this belief you should derive a sense of hope and control over the social engagement process of leadership and your effectiveness.

Influence and Integrity

An individual's life does not exist in isolation from others. The way in which we choose to live our lives will exert an influence, for good or otherwise. The ripple effects of actions taken fan out into an area of life or interaction long after that event or situation has occurred. A good leader influences others by modelling effective leadership characteristics. Good leadership always entails a strong sense of personal values and a desire to transmit these through example.

Just let us take a step back briefly and consider both you, the leader, and your team as human beings. As humans we all have needs and motivation to satisfy these needs. Human needs have been broadly categorised as falling into four areas: physical, mental, emotional/ social and spiritual (Covey et al., 1994). Physical relates to health, home and work/career. Mental relates to thought processes and educational development. Emotional/social relates to social interactions with family, friends and community, which also includes work. The final need is spiritual and relates to finding meaning in something greater than ourselves. For a successful, meaningful life each of these four areas requires our attention for development and growth. Our life, in effect, is about developing these capacities in ourselves. The development of ourselves to be the very best version we can be is best done by aligning such actions with time-honoured values and principles (Covey et al., 1994) that transcend those of just self-serving. Such an adoption of a higher set of values and principles leads to a higher quality of life. If such an approach is adopted by you as a leader your power to influence by acting from a place of integrity cannot but have a positive effect on your team and as a result enhance the engagement of your team.

The art of good leadership is to act and come from a place of high integrity. This is a place of wholeness as a person with the interaction of physical, mental, emotional and spiritual dimensions fully engaged and operating from the highest point. From this place of wholeness self and others are considered in relation to ensuring the best possible outcome for all. It is a place where selfish ego is subdued and yields to a higher set of values being engaged.

THE CARE OF LEADER IDENTITY, INFLUENCE AND INTEGRITY

Consider carefully the below questions and statements and then use the space provided to write down your answers.

Leader Identity – Perception

- Do you see and think of yourself as a leader?
- Have you consciously chosen to lead?
- Leadership is a choice – it is not a position. What are your feelings on this statement?
- How do you think you are doing as a leader? Are there any changes you would like to make? Comment below.

_____
_____
_____
_____
_____
_____
_____
_____
_____
_____
_____
_____

Leader Relational – The Team

- Do you think that others in the team should have a say in the way things are done?
- To what degree do you expect team members to structure their work in order to achieve the unit's goals?
- If members of your team were asked to comment on your leadership what do you think their comments might be? Would this be true of all members of the team?

_____
_____
_____

_____
_____
_____
_____
_____
_____
_____
_____
_____

Leader Dominance – Using Your Position of Power

- How do you lead? Do you use your position of power to get things done by team members?
- In what situations have you resorted to using your status to get things done?
- What has been the reaction of team members to this style?
- Where have you not used your position of power to move things forward? What were the consequences? Would you do anything differently now?

_____
_____
_____
_____
_____
_____
_____
_____
_____
_____
_____

Leader Development

- Do you believe that leadership can be taught?
- What are the areas, if any, that you need to develop as a leader?

_____
_____
_____
_____
_____
_____
_____
_____
_____
_____
_____
_____

Influence and Integrity

- Have you taken time to review the effects of your communications and behaviours on your team members?
- What actions have you taken that are less than your best effort?
- What situations cause you to deliver less than your best?
- Have you operated from a place of high integrity with all your team members or do you view some as less worthy?
- How do you rate your influential skills in relation to senior management? To your peers? What do you need to do more of to become more effective?
- Have you created the appropriate divides between work and home life to operate from your highest point?
- Have you really invested time in influencing others appropriately or do you just carry on without due regard to this?
- Can it be said of you that you can be depended on to tell the truth regardless of circumstances?
- Do you take responsibility for your own actions rather than blame others?

_____
_____
_____
_____
_____
_____

_____

_____

_____

_____

_____

_____

Values

- What values do you hold dear? Are you truly embracing and living from these values?
- Which of these values do you find difficult to consistently hold? *Knowledge, leadership, power, self-development, personal growth, fear of failure, recognition – advancement, financial security – material possessions, challenge, competitiveness, career fulfilment, task accomplishment, enjoyable work, deadlines, client satisfaction, business growth, team spirit, support, helping others, creative imagination*

_____

_____

_____

_____

_____

_____

_____

_____

_____

_____

_____

COMMITMENT TO TAKE ACTION

Before completing this final section take the time to review what you have written up to now. Then create a space, some quiet time, for you to really connect with yourself and see what you truly want to commit to.

For this process stay out of your head as much as possible and instead connect with your heart. Ask of it what is best for you at this time to commit to. When you are ready, take up to three actions to work on over the coming months.

Set these as goals in SMART format, ensuring that you include specific details on the actions necessary. You also will need to measure your progress so decide on the measurement and the frequency for each undertaking. Then transfer these actions and goals to your regular working documents, e.g. your diary.

Finally, before leaving this chapter please sign and date your commitment to these actions below.

Chapter 2 – Identity (Leader Identity): Goal I

_____

_____

_____

_____

_____

Chapter 2 – Identity (Leader Identity): Goal 2

_____

_____

_____

_____

_____

Chapter 2 – Identity (Leader Identity): Goal 3

_____

_____

_____

_____

_____

Sign and Date

_____   _____

3

HOPE

HUMOUR

'Hope is the thing with feathers that perches in the soul, and sings the tunes without the words, and never stops at all.'

Emily Dickinson

Introduction

This third chapter introduces hope, an essential ingredient to have in navigating our journey through life. Humour, a valued running mate, is also included.

Hope

So what is hope? This may be difficult to put into words but let's have a go anyway. Hope could be described as having a positive outlook to life and moving through life optimistically: 'Life is okay now and the future will also be okay.' It is about having faith in yourself that you can negotiate your way through life. You can handle the difficult passages that life may bring as well as the elation that goes with the ups of life. Hope also carries with it the belief that you have a degree of power in making things happen and choice in influencing a situation. It also means that you have the power to create your own scripts. It is optimism 'plus' – the plus being the belief that you can create your own life to realise desired goals. Hopeful people are realistic: they know where they are going, they see the options of different paths and they also understand that getting to where they want may necessitate manoeuvring around obstacles which might be encountered along the way.

Being hopeful and having an optimistic attitude to life and work can be hugely empowering. Hopeful people engage with life rather than run from it. With hope each day can be welcomed as having new beginnings, presenting new opportunities and new possibilities. Hopeful people believe that they meet life as is presented to them and feel that they are in control of their life. They take responsibility for those areas directly in their control, and influence those over which they do not. The mind-set of a hopeful person is of being master of their world rather than a victim.

As a leader you have the potential power to inspire your team, not only by modelling hope but also by creating space and opportunity so that this belief system can take hold with your team, thereby creating a fertile environment and thus facilitating the process of growth – allowing higher performance and success.

When leaders are operating at their best they are potent sources of positive energy. They communicate effectively, have the solutions to the issue and know what to say to influence, inspire and reassure their team. They avoid negative thinking and seek ways of getting their teams to work effectively as a cohesive unit.

From an academic perspective, there is increasing interest in the area of Positive Organisational Behaviour. Luthans (2002, p. 59) defines Positive Organisational Behaviour as 'the study and application of positively oriented human resource strengths and psychological capacities that can be measured, developed, and effectively managed for performance improvement in today's workplace.'

Hope, optimism and resilience were three capacities of Positive Organisational Behaviour studied by Youssef and Luthans (2007) which have a noteworthy impact on performance within organisations. The study demonstrated that hope positively impacted on job satisfaction, work happiness, performance and organisational commitment.

Hope is defined as 'a positive motivational state that is based on an interactively derived sense of successful (1) agency (goal-directed energy) and (2) pathways (planning to meet goals)' (Snyder, Irving and Anderson, 1991, p. 287). Using this definition, Youssef and Luthans (2007, p. 778) argue that 'hope's agency or "willpower" component provides the determination to achieve goals, whereas its pathways or "waypower" component promotes the creation of alternative paths to replace those that may have been blocked in the process of pursuing those goals.'

Setting challenging or 'stretch' goals, contingency planning and redefining goals when necessary to avoid false hope (Luthans, Avey, Avolio, Norman and Combs, 2006; Snyder, 2000) have been identified as practical ways for developing hope.

According to Fredrickson (2001, 2003), positive emotions are beneficial to solving problems concerning personal growth and development. Problem-solving skills, adaptive mechanisms and thought–action repertories can all be enhanced. Further, positive emotion can lead to states of mind which can support an individual, for example by finding positive meaning within adversity and by effective problem-solving.

Humour

'Humour is one of the truly elegant defenses in the human repertoire. Few would deny that the capacity for humour, like hope, is one of mankind's most potent antidotes for the woes of Pandora's Box.'

George Vaillant

Humour, at an individual level, can be viewed as an important coping skill that involves an individual's thoughts, feelings and behaviours. Humour may be seen in many forms: a funny story, a practical joke or a skit. As a coping mechanism it can be seen as an expression of optimism and hope. Humour is a great antidote to stress. It is not a gift that either you have or not. It is a skill and like any skill it needs practice. An interesting way to develop your use of humour is to create appropriate affirmations or indeed to affirm your need for humour. For example, *'I see the humorous side of things, and I have a great sense of humor.'* To illustrate affirmations further, take another example on 'hope', the main topic of this chapter: *'Hope is the substance that defines my successes in life'.*

In organisations today the work environment can be stressful and individuals can become increasingly too serious. Seriousness is a form of fear, breeding anxiety and creating tension which can affect the body, mind and spirit. Humour breaks up seriousness and the build-up of tension. It is a form of play which revitalises us.

In a work environment occasionally dipping into humour shows the lighter side of your humanity to your teams. It also has the potential to show that you are one of the team – 'we are all in it together' so to speak. It also conveys the message that despite the fact that your roles are different that this need not necessarily keep you, the leader, apart from your followers. It may also have the added benefit of relieving unexpressed tension within the team and act as a powerful antidote to stressful situations. Examples of such situations include a difficult project with tight deadlines landing unexpectedly on a department, or a role or responsibility change at the individual or team level. At an organisational level, mergers or downsizing can present hugely challenging times with uncertainty being a significant stressful ingredient.

THE CARE OF HOPE AND HUMOUR

Consider carefully the below questions and statements and then use the space provided to write down your answers.

Hope

- Have you allowed yourself the gift of hope?
- If someone was to describe you would they say you are a hopeful person?
- What do you need to do for yourself to rekindle your sense of hope?
- Do you have this sense of hope at work?
- Does your communication instil a sense of hope in your team members when the going gets tough?
- Is your language around problem situations framed in positive or negative terminology? If you analysed your communications do you more frequently reframe problems as challenges and opportunities for learning or do you state them in negative terms?
- Do you ever use your meetings as a platform for building hope in your team members? For example, do team members have the opportunity to say what is good about what they are doing or what they see as valuable in each other as team members?
- As you lead your team do you create a sense of hope that they will get opportunities to grow and develop and have a chance to use their creativity and talents?
- Where have you created opportunity recently for the members of your team to shine?

_____
_____
_____
_____
_____
_____
_____
_____
_____
_____
_____
_____

Humour

- Is your approach to your life and also your work lacking in humour?
- Is there some unwritten rule at work which necessitates you donning a serious and heavy personality all the time, particularly in your interactions with your team?
- Do you frown on being light-hearted and humorous occasionally? Do you feel that it is not becoming of a leader?
- What are your fears around being humorous?
- In what circumstances could you introduce a bit more humour into your work or life? What are your opportunities for doing so?
- What benefits would this have for your team?
- Are you willing to chance a bit of a change?
- When was the last time you saw a funny movie or listened to a comedian?
- Why do you take yourself so seriously?

_____

_____

_____

_____

_____

_____

_____

_____

_____

_____

_____

COMMITMENT TO TAKE ACTION

Before completing this final section take the time to review what you have written up to now. Then create a space, some quiet time, for you to really connect with yourself and see what you truly want to commit to.

For this process stay out of your head as much as possible and instead connect with your heart. Ask of it what is best for you at this time to commit to. When you are ready, take up to three actions to work on over the coming months.

Set these as goals in SMART format, ensuring that you are including specific details on the actions necessary. You also will need to measure your progress so decide on the measurement and the frequency for each undertaking. Then transfer these actions and goals to your regular working documents, e.g. your diary.

Finally, before leaving this chapter please sign and date your commitment to these actions below.

Chapter 3 – Hope: Goal 1

_____
_____
_____
_____
_____

Chapter 3 – Hope: Goal 2

_____
_____
_____
_____
_____

Chapter 3 – Hope: Goal 3

_____

_____

_____

_____

_____

Sign and Date

_____   _____

4

SEEKING OUT

SELF-ESTEEM

'The voyage of discovery is not in seeking new landscapes but in having new eyes.'

Marcel Proust

Introduction

This chapter on 'seeking out' embraces two aspects: feedback and opportunities to learn. These elements provide pathways through which you can expand and develop your potential. Self-esteem is viewed as a significant enabler of this process and as a determinant of the degree to which you are willing to seek out; it will also merit attention in this chapter.

Seeking Out Feedback

Leadership is essentially a social interaction with the leader and the followers (the team) being the two sides of the leadership process coin. The phrase 'without followers there can be no leaders' is nowhere more relevant than in implicit leadership theories, the everyday images people hold of what a leader is. An individual, whether this is the leader or the follower, is at the heart of leadership as it is the individual's perspectives which need to be addressed when viewing the leadership process and its development.

Leadership effectiveness and therefore your success as a leader may be best viewed through this lens of the social context. The follower is a key ingredient in these social context interactions. Their reactions and actions towards you are of prime importance, providing signals on whether they have accepted you as the leader or not, i.e. the 'granting' aspect of the leadership process. Inputs to your followers can be distilled to thoughts, which in turn influence the feelings and behaviours of that individual in their interactions with you. Continued perceptions of situations where leaders are viewed as effective or ineffective are many and constantly reinforce or alter the contents of implicit leadership theories, and the followers' view on whether you are matching up to these images.

The leader is one side of the social interaction coin and, as has been discussed in Chapter 2, the leader must feel firstly that he/she is the leader and as a consequence hold a strong leader identity – the 'claiming' aspect to the leadership process. As a leader, at the very least you should be a bit curious to learn more about how you are viewed by your followers and whether your actions and behaviours are a good match to what your followers deem a good leader to be. Furthermore, as your actions span out into the wider organisation it would be beneficial to get soundings about your effectiveness in this wider arena. Seeking feedback and gathering views on your effectiveness from both your followers and key personnel within your sphere of influence may be seen as a wise and brave move. Changing and acting more effectively where appropriate is the expected response to such feedback.

Feedback availability from the organisation may be viewed as having two aspects: the 'job itself' and 'people'. The job itself relates to feedback from the actual mechanics of the job, demonstrating whether the activity was done correctly or otherwise. Take performance management with a leader having four direct reports and the organisational requirement to perform formal, semi-annual performance reviews. In this instance the evidence of feedback regarding the job itself would be that eight performance review meetings were conducted within the year and there were eight supporting signed-off reports. The second aspect of feedback availability relates to people. In that performance management example, in the meetings held the quality and effectiveness of the exchange between the leader and follower is the social context of leadership. This 'people' aspect is central and considered an important determinant in leader and leadership development.

Seeking Out Opportunities to Learn

Another gauge of leadership development is the capacity to actively seek opportunities to gain more knowledge or learn new skills to further develop and integrate the learning into your role. Inherent in any learning process is the potential for making mistakes. As a leader, your attitude towards handling mistakes and your ability to respond effectively to setbacks become another important element of this.

If a leader were to rigidly hold the notion of perfection at all costs then intolerance to mistakes would be the dominant attitude. In such an environment mistakes would be viewed only as weaknesses and with it the potential opportunity to learn would become stifled. With such a rigid view – that perfect outcomes with perfect results are the only acceptable output – growth can be stunted. Fear is fostered in such environments, which in turn breeds inflexibility. This is coupled with the closing down of ideas and opportunities for learning and making improvements. This approach also sets the standard for mediocrity, favouring zero tolerance for change, with its potential for improvements, and opportunities for learning and growth are lost. Such organisational cultures cut off the life force for creativity and development.

'The capacity to learn is a gift; the ability to learn is a skill; the willingness to learn is a choice.'

Brian Herbert, author

Self-Esteem

Self-esteem is crucial to a person's survival in the world, and nowhere is it more important than in the leadership environment. It is extremely important to develop healthy self-esteem to have a happy and productive life. Without healthy self-esteem life can be viewed and experienced in a sea of fear. Opportunities for embracing life and expanding and developing from them are severely retarded or missed out completely. Both seeking out feedback and the opportunities to learn, as discussed above, become shut down or very rarely engaged in a person of low self-esteem.

In motivational terms, self-esteem is viewed as one of the two growth and expansion needs according to Maslow's (1943) hierarchy of needs; the second relates to self-actualisation. These two growth needs differ from the three lower-order needs of physiological needs, security and belonging, which are viewed as dependence needs.

Self-esteem relates to growth and arises from within. It has been referred to as the fourth stressor but we have immense control over it. Low self-esteem can plague the lives of individuals from early childhood to the grave, robbing them of the experience of life and reducing them to living a half-life in the shadow of what could be. They live with the constant chatter of a critic sitting on their shoulder watching their every move, waiting ever-ready to pounce and tell them that they are not good enough or deserving enough. This constant plaguing by the critic causes people to give up and leads them to selling themselves short. The critic drives them to walk out on themselves and on who they really are, abandoning their hopes and dreams.

Self-esteem development begins with our family and is a product of our life experiences. It has been shown that parent–child interaction fosters 'stress hardiness' – the ability to cope with stress. Maddi and Kobasa (1984), in their book *The Hardy Executive: Health under Stress*, as cited by Benson and Stuart (1993), point out that that the messages that stress-hardy individuals received in their past were ones which had an emphasis on reward, not punishment. This built commitment as opposed to alienisation. The tasks given to them were moderate in difficulty. This built feelings of control rather that powerlessness. Further, they were encouraged to look at ongoing changes as full of possibilities, thus allowing them to feel challenged rather than threatened. Such individuals develop healthy self-esteem.

Looking further, healthy self-esteem is about believing statements like the following:

- I am ok with me – I am ok with the good parts and equally so I am ok with the not so good parts.
- I am accepting of myself exactly as I am.
- I love myself just exactly as I am, warts and all.

Having healthy self-esteem is like treating yourself as you would treat a best friend. People with healthy self-esteem like their own company and above all they can accept themselves. It also means that you would not sell yourself out when mistakes are made or because of your shortcomings. It means that with awareness you have growth opportunities, that you can learn from your mistakes rather than be ashamed and view yourself as undesirable.

THE CARE OF SEEKING OUT

Consider carefully the below questions and statements and then use the space provided to write down your answers.

Seeking Out Feedback

- Do you take all feedback seriously or do you simply dismiss it?
- Do you pursue feedback from people even if they are reluctant to give it?
- Do you approach people to inquire about your impact on them?
- Do you willingly seek help from others in an effort to improve yourself?
- Do you talk openly about your mistakes?
- Are you open to criticism about yourself?
- Do you reflect on the feedback you have been given?

_____
_____
_____
_____
_____
_____
_____
_____
_____
_____
_____
_____

Seeking Out Opportunities to Learn

- Over the last couple of months have you actively sought out any new opportunities to learn? Did these provide a potential that may have changed your perspective or an opportunity to learn new things? Do you actively seek opportunities to learn and expand your knowledge and skills?
- Is it more true that you seek out opportunities to learn or that projects are imposed on you?

- How do you view mistakes – mistakes which you make and also the mistakes of others?
- Identify a mistake which you made in the last month. What can you say you have learned from it? Did you change direction as a result of this mistake?
- How would you describe your attitude to setbacks?
- Do you respond effectively to feedback?
- Do you appear brittle to criticism?
- Where or what have you changed as a result of feedback?

_____
_____
_____
_____
_____
_____
_____
_____
_____
_____
_____
_____

Self-Esteem Questionnaire

For this section take the opportunity to review the internet for a questionnaire on self-esteem. For example, Rosenberg's (1965) Self-Esteem Scale (RSE) has ten items on a self-report measure of self-esteem. Once completed, review the results and add any insights in the section below.

_____
_____
_____
_____
_____
_____
_____
_____

_____

_____

_____

Self-Esteem – You as Leader

- Do you work hard because you enjoy it and are committed to it?
- Do you believe that you can construct your life by making decisions and implementing them?
- Do you approach the future enthusiastically because the changes it will bring seem potentially worthwhile and you see them as challenges?
- Can you face an issue where you might feel insecure, and have the courage to bring it out into the open so you can examine what needs to be done?
- What are the thoughts that you hold about yourself/about a given issue? What steps must you take to challenge them?
- Do you really believe in yourself?

_____

_____

_____

_____

_____

_____

_____

_____

_____

_____

_____

_____

Self-Esteem – Your Interaction with Your Followers

- Do you make individual roles as interesting as possible?
- Do you allow your followers the flexibility to have inputs into their roles?
- Do you delegate where you can or do you still feel you have to control everything?

- Do you support your followers with the necessary tools and knowledge for their roles? Do you coach and mentor them to develop their talents and create an environment which fosters their self-esteem? Or do you punish them with a too-quick putdown and diminish their confidence in order to feel better or superior?
- Do you single people out as in the situation described above? What is it in them that you see as unworthy? What is it in them that you so dislike?

_____

_____

_____

_____

_____

_____

_____

_____

_____

_____

_____

COMMITMENT TO TAKE ACTION

Before completing this final section take the time to review what you have written up to now. Then create a space, some quiet time, for you to really connect with yourself and see what you truly want to commit to.

For this process, stay out of your head as much as possible and instead connect with your heart. Ask of it what is best for you at this time to commit to. When you are ready, take up to three actions to work on over the coming months.

Set these as goals in SMART format, ensuring that you are including specific details on the actions necessary. You also will need to measure your progress so decide on the measurement and the frequency for each undertaking. Then transfer these actions and goals to your regular working documents, e.g. your diary.

Finally, before leaving this chapter please sign and date your commitment to these actions below.

Chapter 4 – Seeking Out: Goal 1

_____

_____

_____

_____

_____

Chapter 4 – Seeking Out: Goal 2

_____

_____

_____

_____

_____

Chapter 4 – Seeking Out: Goal 3

_____

_____

_____

_____

_____

Sign and Date

_____   _____

5

RESPONSIBILITY

RESULTS

'We are made wise not by the recollection of our past, but by the responsibility for our future.'

George Bernard Shaw

Introduction

Responsibility may be viewed as a hybrid of two words – 'response' and 'ability'. Responsibility as a human capacity which sets us apart from the rest of the animal kingdom is the theme of this chapter, and with it the linked topic of results. Results may be viewed as a direct output of our responses. In viewing results we can change situations by choosing to adopt different actions which will alter the outcome. We have responsibility and freedom to choose and with that comes the notion that there are consequences for our choices.

Responsibility

As humans we have the ability to respond to any and all situations in life. As adults this is a given. Many of us may argue to the contrary and wish to continue with the delusion that we are not responsible, preferring to look outside of ourselves for decisions and answers, and also looking outside to blame others. But we are in charge of our lives, nobody else is. The simple fact is that we are masters of our own lives.

Responsibility

Our lives – the good and equally the bad parts – are products of ourselves and what we have created. Every situation in our environment has been drawn into us as we have created it. We are constantly creating events and situations, both positive and negative, and we do so consciously or unconsciously – grand or small, the size makes no difference – we have created all of them. Obviously, those that are positive and pleasurable are fine for us while those of a negative nature are unwanted by us. However, the negative ones are our creations too.

Emotions play a significant part in our life; we are emotional beings. Emotional intelligence is a vital element of successful survival in life and will be dealt with in Chapter 6, so emotions here will only be discussed as they relate to the subject of responsibility. Emotions are our driving force and operate as an excellent barometer of our satisfaction or otherwise of our life. Being aware of your emotional state is beneficial so that you can take appropriate action as necessary to create or restore desired states once you become aware of unwanted course deviation. Here are some interesting questions for you to mull over:

- Who or what is in the driving seat of your life now? Are emotions driving you or are you driving them?
- Do you find that your emotional state is disturbed when in the company of others who are very emotionally charged?

It is important to understand, indeed to recognise, who is in the driving seat in your life. You can now become more aware and be more powerfully conscious in your life and draw to you only what you want and eliminate what is unhelpful and unwanted. It is your responsibility to create the environment or situation which you want. It is equally valid to state that your emotional state is your responsibility.

For any situation in which you find yourself you should check on and be conscious of your emotional state. If you discover that you are emotionally upset then you need to take responsibility for yourself and your emotions. After all, you have created them. The events and the people involved in the situation are acting as mere mirrors for you to view yourself and your emotions. If you wind up getting emotional about the events of the situation, then the issues which are triggering these emotions will require you to deal with them. You need to own these emotions, take responsibility for them as yours, not the other person's.

Too often there is a tendency to blame the other person rather than face up to them. You are responsible for your environment and your emotional state. You need to ensure that you are owning your part of it and taking charge. For you not to do this is handing your power away and thus placing yourself in the victim role. In this victim role you are held prisoner-like, continually lashing out and blaming the other person or events. In these negative cycles you are kept stuck, drained of energy; you are depleting positivity and condemn yourself to victimhood. You are choosing stuck-ness rather than taking responsibility and ownership for the situation, learning from it and mastering emotions and moving forward.

'You must take personal responsibility. You cannot change the circumstances, the seasons, or the wind, but you can change yourself. That is something you have charge of.'

Jim Rohn

In any situation, regardless of the circumstances, there is always something you can do to move the situation forward to influence the events. It means focusing energy and attention on what you can change and not wasting energy on and becoming frustrated with the things over which you do not have control. So rather than adopting a hopeless, helpless attitude, by viewing the enormity of the issue you can change your focus. Such a switch in focus requires you to take responsibility for and action in the areas over which you can have direct control. By engaging your effort and energies on only these areas you can exert a positive influence on the issue and thereby improve the outcome. Engaging such approaches frequently cements the 'response-ability' capability of us humans and fosters growth and development.

Life does not act on you. You can influence your environment by choosing and taking action to create an empowering life. With the choice of action you need to realise that there are consequences – so conscious choice in your thoughts and emotions is a wise response if you want to have mastery of your life. Moving into your personal power changes your life and you make things happen for you. You are no longer stuck in the belief that circumstances out there require changing before you can move on, get what you want. Life is a reflection of all inner beliefs. The choice is yours to be victim or master. I am reminded of the words from *A Course in Miracles* (Schucman, Thetford and Wapnick, 2007):

Somehow we must develop faith
And trust in our Self.
Anything the mind can conceive and believe, the mind can 'achieve'.
The thought manifests as the word,
The word manifests as the deed.
The deed manifests into habit.
And the habit hardens into character.
So watch the thought and the way with care!

Results

'As you sow, so shall you reap.' Results are the proof of your actions. It is a wise person who builds in a reflective segment at the end part of any process to investigate whether the desired result was achieved or not and also to review the process employed to get there.

What may be interesting to reflect on is the approach adopted and whether the intention was to achieve the result at any cost. Oftentimes we can get so blinded with tunnel vision focus on the results that the 'how' of getting there is treated as insignificant or ignored. With such an approach working relationships, including your followers' development, can play a poor second fiddle in the rush of getting to the end line.

THE CARE OF RESPONSIBILITY AND RESULTS

Consider carefully the below questions and statements and then use the space provided to write down your answers.

Responsibility

- In your role as leader what do you believe is your responsibility in influencing others?
- Do the company goals and values resonate with you? What action do you wish to take, if any?
- How do you take responsibility to live these values in your daily interactions with staff and peers?
- Are you taking responsibility for your unit's effective functioning despite any of the obstacles what may be encountered along the way?
- How do you respond in the face of obstacles?
- How frequently do you blame situations or people for events in your unit?
- What is preventing you from stepping into your personal power right now and taking full responsibility for your life?
- Where have you not taken responsibility today? As you reflect on this, what would you do differently?
- What plans are you putting in place to make taking responsibility a more permanent feature in your life?

_____

_____

_____

_____

_____

_____

_____

_____

_____

_____

_____

_____

Results

- Do you pay due attention to achieving your unit's goals and targets?
- Do you continually miss the target date, believing instead to just deliver as best you can? Do you actually hold yourself responsible for each of the goals?
- Where have you shielded yourself and blamed circumstances and others for not achieving the desired results?
- Do you get too focused on results at the expense of the process and journey? What has been the price of this approach?
- Have you lost your credibility as a leader for your approach? What can you do to restore this?

_____

_____

_____

_____

_____

_____

_____

_____

_____

_____

_____

_____

COMMITMENT TO TAKE ACTION

Before completing this final section take the time to review what you have written up to now. Then create a space, some quiet time, for you to really connect with yourself and see what you truly want to commit to.

For this process, stay out of your head as much as possible and instead connect with your heart. Ask of it what is best for you at this time to commit to. When you are ready, take up to three actions to work on over the coming months.

Set these as goals in SMART format, ensuring that you are including specific details on the actions necessary. You also will need to measure your progress so decide on the measurement and the frequency for each undertaking. Then transfer these actions and goals to your regular working documents, e.g. your diary.

Finally, before leaving this chapter please sign and date your commitment to these actions below.

Chapter 5 – Responsibility: Goal 1

_____
_____
_____
_____
_____

Chapter 5 – Responsibility: Goal 2

_____
_____
_____
_____
_____

Chapter 5 – Responsibility: Goal 3

_____

_____

_____

_____

_____

Sign and Date

_____   _____

6

EMOTIONAL INTELLIGENCE (EI)

'If your emotional abilities aren't in hand, if you don't have self-awareness, if you are not able to manage your distressing emotions, if you can't have empathy and have effective relationships, then no matter how smart you are, you are not going to get very far.'

Daniel Goleman

Introduction

In today's world we see daily examples of people lashing out emotionally, making decisions and running their lives on the simple basis of how they feel. This chapter introduces the subject of emotional intelligence (EI), a topic which has gained significant importance since the 1990s. EI moves beyond the confines of intellectual quotient (IQ) and the notion that the latter is the totality of human intelligence and that once issued with a certain capacity it cannot be altered. EI also provides us with the answers as to why some people with high IQ flounder in life, while others with only a medium IQ fare out well. Furthermore, EI presents us with the hope that the EI component capacities can be learned and therefore expanded.

Emotional Intelligence

The primal dimension of leadership, emotional intelligence, the subject matter of this chapter, is intrinsically linked to the identity of the leader and leadership development. For successful leadership you need to be intelligent about your emotions. This pivotal ingredient requires you to be self- and socially aware and also to manage both of these dimensions.

Emotional Intelligence (EI)

Emotional intelligence may be defined as the ability to perceive emotions, to access and generate emotions to assist thought, to understand emotions and emotional knowledge, and to reflectively regulate emotions so as to promote emotional and intellectual growth (Mayer and Salovey, 1997, p. 10).

At least four major aspects are associated with emotional intelligence: the appraisal and expression of emotion, the use of emotion to enhance cognitive processes and decision-making, knowledge about emotions, and the management of emotions, all of which are related. The more generally described aspects to EI, as presented by Goleman, Boyatzis and McKee (2002) are encapsulated in the four elements of self-awareness, self-management, social awareness and relationship management.

EI has many benefits and can lead to enhanced functioning in achievement. There is a close relationship between EI and the leader–follower interaction as EI is interlinked with identity and the claiming (by the leader) and granting (by the follower) of leadership.

As a leader, you may use your emotions to enhance your information processing of challenges, threats and opportunities. Accurately appraising how your followers currently feel, relying on your knowledge of emotions to understand why they feel this way, and influencing followers' emotions so that they are receptive and supportive of your goals are key to a leader and leadership. Self-awareness is part of leader development while social awareness relates to leadership development.

Goleman (1998), in his book *Working with Emotional Intelligence*, provides a framework of personal competencies to develop outstanding performance which stem from EI. The skills, totalling twenty-five in all, are spread across the five domains of self-awareness, self-regulation, motivation, empathy and social skills. Goleman (1998) emphasises that it is not necessary to gain perfection in all. Acknowledging the fact that people have different strengths and limitations, he suggests that developing typically six or so of these qualities across the five domains is sufficient to develop outstanding performance.

Self-awareness competencies are comprised of emotional self-awareness, accurate self-assessment and self-confidence. Social awareness or empathy encompasses understanding others, developing others, service orientation, leveraging diversity, and political awareness. Self-awareness has been declared as the 'first commandment' of EI. Leader development is largely personal development, which is the process of becoming more aware of yourself. Identities can be sharpened by raising self-awareness, which is critical for leader development and success in the leadership process.

Having become both self- and socially aware you must now take the action necessary to ground this knowledge in practicality and make a positive impact. This is achieved through the dimensions of self-regulation (self-management), motivation and social skills (relationship management). Firstly, self-regulation or self-management is supported through the competencies of self-control, trustworthiness, conscientiousness, adaptability and innovation, coupled with the motivational competencies of commitment, optimism, initiative and drive (Goleman, 1998). Secondly, the dimension of social skills or relationship management is supported by the competencies of influence, communication, conflict management, leadership, change catalyst, building bonds, collaboration and cooperation, and team capabilities (Goleman, 1998).

Effective leaders act through emotions, for example in painting an organisational vision of leading and assuring their team in times of uncertainty. It has been said that leaders act on the group and have the capacity to sway people's emotions. So if people's emotions are driven in a positive fashion, performance will excel, as the best in everyone will come to the fore. The key to making leadership work is to engage and become proficient in at least one of the competencies within each dimension of the emotional intelligence framework. You need to become proficient in handling yourself and also your relationships. What is crucial in this context is not just what you do but more importantly how it is done. Research shows that emotions spread with people in groups inevitably catching feelings from one another. This sharing applies to the full emotional spectrum. The degree of cohesiveness of the group determines how quickly and effectively the emotions are shared. Generally speaking, it is the leader who adds the strongest emotions to the group. The leader's emotional reaction is viewed as the most valid response by the group. As a leader, your act of giving or withholding praise, criticism or support to each person's contribution, allowing flexibility and freedom in doing the job, helps determine their primal emotional impact. If you were to lack credibility as the leader your followers would turn to someone else whom they trust and respect for emotional guidance. Your proficiency in transmitting determines the potency of emotions to spread. The more enthusiastic you are the more readily your followers will catch on to this. Emotions have real consequences affecting getting work done and achieving the desired results.

Emotional Intelligence versus Intelligence Quotient

Goleman et al. (2002) analysed data from nearly 500 global companies to determine which personal capabilities drove outstanding performance. They recognised that intellect, to some degree, was a driver of outstanding performance and that cognitive abilities (big-picture thinking and vision) are important; both are IQ related. However, they state that the ingredients which 'distinguished outstanding leaders revealed that EI based competencies played an increasingly important role at higher levels of organisation, where technical differences were negligible' and that 'the higher the rank of those considered star performers, the more EI competencies emerged as the reason for their effectiveness' (Goleman et al., 2002, p. 250). In fact, EI factors were attributed to account for 85 per cent of the difference between the 'star performers' and average performers. Intellectual abilities are required to obtain jobs, with 'high selection pressure for IQ to enter the executive ranks and relatively little variation in IQ among those who are in those ranks' (Goleman et al., 2002, p. 250); however, 'EI contributes 80–90 percent of the competencies that distinguish outstanding from average leaders' (Goleman et al., 2002, p. 251).

THE CARE OF EMOTIONAL INTELLIGENCE

Consider carefully the below questions and statements and then use the space provided to write down your answers.

Self-Awareness

Emotional Self-Awareness

- Are you aware of your inner signals?
- What feelings do you have right now?
- What feelings did you have during your last interaction with a direct report whose performance was weak?
- What emotions do you generally have with each member of your team? Are these different or similar? And if so, why?
- What do you do/say to yourself when you display some negative emotions in relation to something you did or think which was linked to a particular emotion?
- As you reflect back over the last month select one example of a challenge which you faced. Is there anything you would do differently with this benefit of hindsight? Specify.
- What damage was done to you and/or others in the last incident where you did not handle your emotional state well?

_____

_____

_____

_____

_____

_____

_____

_____

_____

_____

_____

_____

Accurate Self-Assessment

- What are your strengths? What is the evidence to support these?
- What are your limitations? What is the evidence to support these?
- What do you need to improve upon? How do you feel about this? Truly?

_____

_____

_____

_____

_____

_____

_____

_____

_____

_____

_____

Self-Confidence

- How would you describe your level of confidence?
- If your direct reports were approached and asked about their confidence in you as their leader what do you think they would say? Why would that be so?

_____

_____

_____

_____

_____

_____

_____

_____

_____

_____

_____

Self-Regulation (Self-Management)

Self-Control

- How would you describe your emotional state in the last stressful event or trying situation you faced?
- Would others say that you remained calm and clear-headed?

_____

_____

_____

_____

_____

_____

_____

_____

_____

_____

Trustworthiness

- Do you live all the values which you espouse?
- Would others at work say that you are open about your feelings, beliefs and actions?
- Do you admit to your mistakes?
- What actions do you take when confronted with unethical behaviour in others, regardless of their position within the organisation?

_____

_____

_____

_____

_____

_____

_____

_____

_____

_____

Conscientiousness

Read the following statements and comment on how true they are for you:

- I am a person with high standards and I apply them consistently to both myself and my team.
- I am alert to opportunities to improve performance.

_____
_____
_____
_____
_____
_____
_____
_____
_____
_____
_____
_____

Adaptability

- When faced with multiple demands does this drain you of energy? Do you lose your focus?
- How would you describe your comfort level with handling ambiguities and conflicting demands within your organisation?
- Do you consider yourself flexible in adapting to new challenges? Is this opinion shared also by your supervisor?

_____
_____
_____
_____
_____
_____
_____
_____
_____

_____
_____
_____

Innovation

Read the following statements and comment on how true they are for you:

- I am willing to take the initiative in most situations.
- I seize opportunities when they are presented or I create them.
- I cut through red tape when necessary to create better possibilities for the future.

_____
_____
_____
_____
_____
_____
_____
_____
_____
_____
_____

Motivational Competencies

Commitment

- Are you truly committed to continuous personal and professional development? Or do you feel that there is very little room for improvement and that you could devote your time to pursuing some other interests?
- What level of commitment do you have for ensuring that the department goals are achieved within the agreed timeframes?

_____
_____

_____
_____
_____
_____
_____
_____
_____
_____
_____
_____

Optimism

- How would you describe your approach to life?
- What attitude do you adopt to challenges?
- Which is more true: you see change as a threat or an opportunity?
- Do you see yourself as a glass half-full or glass half-empty person?
- Do you expect the best out of life?

_____
_____
_____
_____
_____
_____
_____
_____
_____
_____
_____

Initiative

- What initiatives have you taken in the last twelve months that have significantly impacted on your career and on you personally?
- What learnings and encouragement can you take forward with you for this coming year?

_____
_____
_____
_____
_____
_____
_____
_____
_____
_____
_____

Drive

Describe your reaction to setbacks and obstacles. When answering this question reflect on a recent situation. Consider as you reflect on it how committed you were to seeing it through. Comment on any insights you have.

_____
_____
_____
_____
_____
_____
_____
_____
_____
_____
_____

Empathy (Social Awareness)

Understanding Others

Read the following statements and comment on how true they are for you:

- When working with my team I am consciously aware of others' emotions. I can accurately pick up on these emotions, which are often unspoken.
- I actively listen to others to understand their point of view.

_____

_____

_____

_____

_____

_____

_____

_____

_____

_____

_____

_____

Developing Others

- Do you actively and consciously seek out opportunities to develop your followers?
- What has the response of your followers been to these new challenges?
- Have you further supported and encouraged your followers when they were somewhat anxious about the challenge?
- Have you committed to each team member's development over the last twelve months?
- Have you consciously helped them to play to their strengths?

_____

_____

_____

_____

_____

_____

_____

_____

_____

_____

_____

Service Orientation

- What is your awareness of and attitude towards your internal and external customers?
- How frequently do you seek out what your customers need (both internal and external customers)?
- Are surveys for customer satisfaction completed at least annually? Were there any surprises in the last survey? What specific follow-up actions did you take?
- What measures do you take to ensure that your customers' needs are met and satisfied?
- Do you make yourself available to your customers if required?

_____

_____

_____

_____

_____

_____

_____

_____

_____

_____

_____

Leveraging Diversity

Read the following statements and comment on how true they are for you:

- I can get along well in all groups including those with diverse backgrounds and cultures.
- I recognise that having diversity within my team brings a freshness to the thinking process and opens the possibility of bringing novel ways to problem-solving.

_____
_____
_____
_____
_____
_____
_____
_____
_____
_____
_____
_____
_____

Political Awareness

- How good do you think your social awareness and your level of political astuteness is?
- How would you rate your ability to read key power relationships?

_____
_____
_____
_____
_____
_____
_____
_____
_____
_____
_____

Social Skills (Relationship Management)

Influence

- Describe the last time you had to influence others. How did you go about getting buy-in? How persuasive were you?

- How has your emotion influenced the behaviour of someone this week? Has this been a positive or negative experience? If you had your chance all over what would you do differently?

_____
_____
_____
_____
_____
_____
_____
_____
_____
_____
_____
_____

Communication

- How frequently have you shared your vision or the department mission with your team?
- What has been your team's reaction to you sharing the mission?
- Do you actively listen to others to understand their point of view?

_____
_____
_____
_____
_____
_____
_____
_____
_____
_____
_____
_____

Conflict Management

- How comfortable are you with conflict?
- How effectively do you handle conflict?
- Do you encourage members of the team to speak their opinions and ideas even if they are different from yours?
- Are there some members of the team who do not contribute and have you sought out the reasons why? Have any of your actions been responsible for this?

_____
_____
_____
_____
_____
_____
_____
_____
_____
_____
_____
_____

Leadership

- How would you describe your commitment to developing members of your team?
- What actions have you taken in the last six months to develop each of your team members to play to their strengths?
- How much time have you invested in giving prompt and specific feedback to members of your team?
- Do you delegate effectively? Or do you delegate to dump?
- Have you coached team members as required? Where have you fallen down in this regard?

_____
_____
_____
_____
_____

_____
_____
_____
_____
_____
_____
_____

Change Catalyst

- Do you analyse situations and recognise when change is needed?
- Are you comfortable about challenging the status quo when needed?
- Have you taken the time to make compelling arguments for change if needed?

_____
_____
_____
_____
_____
_____
_____
_____
_____
_____
_____
_____

Building Bonds

Read the following statements and comment on how true they are for you:

- I nurture relationships amongst team members.
- My nurturing of relationships is done in alignment with my commitment to the goals of the organisation.

_____
_____

_____
_____
_____
_____
_____
_____
_____
_____
_____
_____

Collaboration and Cooperation

- What methods and strategies do you adopt to ensure that you have an effective team and have excellent collaboration from each member of your team?
- What do you do to build spirit and identity in your team?
- How would you describe the relationship you have with your team?
- How would you describe the relationships that each of the team members have with each other?
- What norms and values have you instilled in the team to create a high-performance teamwork culture?

_____
_____
_____
_____
_____
_____
_____
_____
_____
_____
_____
_____

Team Capabilities

- How effective are you in creating group synergies in pursing collective goals?

_____

_____

_____

_____

_____

_____

_____

_____

_____

_____

_____

COMMITMENT TO TAKE ACTION

Before completing this final section take the time to review what you have written up to now. Then create a space, some quiet time, for you to really connect with yourself and see what you truly want to commit to.

For this process stay out of your head as much as possible and instead connect with your heart. Ask of it what is best for you at this time to commit to. When you are ready, take up to three actions to work on over the coming months.

Set these as goals in SMART format, ensuring that you are including specific details on the actions necessary. You also will need to measure your progress so decide on the measurement and the frequency for each undertaking. Then transfer these actions and goals to your regular working documents, e.g. your diary.

Finally, before leaving this chapter please sign and date your commitment to these actions below.

Chapter 6 – Emotional Intelligence: Goal 1

_____

_____

_____

_____

_____

Chapter 6 – Emotional Intelligence: Goal 2

_____

_____

_____

_____

_____

Chapter 6 – Emotional Intelligence: Goal 3

_____

_____

_____

_____

_____

Sign and Date

_____   _____

7

DEVELOPMENT

DELEGATION

'In the past the man has been first; in the future the system must be first. ... The first object of any good system must be that of developing first-class men.'

Frederick W. Taylor

Introduction

Development is central to the nature of humanity. The leadership process is no different. This chapter discusses development through the lens of delegation and empowerment of individuals and teams. Job design and its effect on motivation are included.

Development

There are many phases of development and growth in the human life cycle, from birth to death. Within the adult development cycle there are critical phases which require successful negotiation of a given phase before advancing to the next. A developmental approach may also be applied to human motivation, with individuals growing and advancing to reach their highest potentials in the development of their capacities. Maslow (1943) addresses human motivational needs development in terms of five ascending levels in his hierarchy of needs. The physiological, on the first level, is the lowest of the three lower-order needs, with security and belonging filling the second and third levels, completing what are also termed the 'dependency' needs. The two higher-order 'growth' needs of self-esteem and self-actualisation then follow. Maslow amended his model near the end of his life to include what he called 'self-transcendence' – a focus on a higher goal outside ourselves – placing self-transcendence as a motivational step beyond self-actualisation (Maslow, 1969). Maslow's theory posits the requirement of satisfying lower-order needs before advancing to the next as the person develops and evolves.

Applying Maslow's (1943) theory to a work context, the physiological need is met through the exchange of labour for money – providing for the basic necessities of food and shelter. The second need, security, can be met by the provision of a safe working environment which includes physical and psychological perspectives. Being part of an organisation, and more particularly a team, provides the ingredients to meet the next need, belonging. Once these are adequately addressed then there is potential to develop the higher-order growth needs of self-esteem and self-actualisation.

Self-esteem relates to how you see yourself – your worth and value. This can be viewed as pride in your work and contribution, on the one hand, and, on the other, having this work recognised by others. Self-esteem has been previously examined in Chapter 4 (Seeking Out). Self-actualisation, the fifth and final need, is concerned with the development of your potential, expressing and developing your capacities and your own uniqueness – your creativity is your gift to the world. There may be many sources drawn upon to support this growth need, with work being only one such contributor.

As a leader, you have a responsibility for the job content of each of your team members. Typically this is reflected in job roles which hopefully will include the provision of stimulating work for your followers. Motivational theories emphasise the need for ensuring that work has meaning and value and that the individual can identify with this. Therefore, work design becomes increasingly more important as it is intricately linked with well-being.

Hackman and Oldham (1976), in their Job Characteristics Theory, propose that high motivation is related to experiencing three psychological states whilst working: meaningfulness of work, responsibility and knowledge of outcomes. Each of these states can be explained as follows. Firstly, meaningfulness of work relates to the work itself, which must be motivating and the individual must relate to it. Secondly, responsibility means that an individual is afforded the opportunity to succeed or otherwise at the job and is given sufficient freedom of action, including the ability to make changes and incorporate the learning gained whilst doing the job. Finally, knowledge of outcomes means that knowledge is provided on how successful an individual's work was whilst also enabling them to learn from their mistakes. In addition, it can connect that individual emotionally to the end user of their product, thereby further fuelling their sense of purpose with their work.

The work must be experienced as meaningful, as previously stated, and must also be seen as the individual's contribution significantly affecting the overall effectiveness of the organisation. In this theory (Hackman and Oldham, 1976), five core job characteristics are identified as impacting on motivation and satisfaction of employees: skill variety (of employees' skills and talents); task identity (referring to the extent to which a job requires completing the whole process from beginning to end); task significance (identifying that the task is contributing to something wider beyond self, benefiting society); responsibility (autonomy derived from the freedom to schedule work and determine how it will be carried out); and knowledge of outcomes (feedback received and the individual gaining awareness of the outcome on the effectiveness of their efforts). This feedback can come from other people or the job itself. Knowing these critical job characteristics, it is then possible to derive the key components of the design of a job and redesign it.

Employees who are more internally motivated and satisfied with their overall job and personal growth opportunities generate high-quality work and have a lower absentee or turnover rate when there is a well-developed job design. This in turn will result in positive work outcomes. Increasing the motivational potential indicates the degree to which jobs are 'enriched' in that they provide for the fulfilment of growth needs (Gardner and Cummings, 1988). Growth needs, in turn, focus on the development of human potential and the desire for personal growth and increased competence (Alderfer, 1969). As the strength of each individual's growth needs is different, you need to get to know each team member's motivational requirement rather than adopting a one-size-fits-all approach.

Delegation

Let me introduce a cautionary note at the outset. Please remember to delegate to develop and not to dump: delegate to motivate.

Delegation goes hand-in-hand with empowering members of your team to grow and develop. Delegating projects to members of your team enables your followers to build skills and strengths. In so doing they are helping the organisation as they increase their value. How many leaders truly believe that by delegating they are not only helping themselves as leaders but also helping their followers, and that this has a direct pay off-for their organisation? The degree to which you manage delegation is proportional to the degree to which you view yourself as a leader, not just a manager. It also reflects the degree of self-confidence which you hold. Equally reflected is the degree to which you, as a leader, hold power and reins over your followers, and this, in my view, can be linked to the degree of fear which you hold. Wanting control and lacking the desire to delegate and develop your followers is a reflection of you being a fearful individual (leader). Fear is reflected in the following beliefs:

- The job will not be done properly to the correct standard.
- It will take too much of my time to train the person up to the task.
- If I delegate this task my role will diminish.

It is your responsibility as a leader to delegate as you are supposed to get results through people. As a leader you are ultimately accountable for any tasks delegated. Having a very clear expectation of the standard of performance is crucial before any delegation takes place.

Effectively communicating the task to be delegated and gaining agreement of your followers is vital. You need to clearly communicate what monitoring steps are required during the process and give assurance of your support over the project. Effective delegation will create more empowered followers, with greater confidence, increased skills and higher degrees of motivation.

Motivation One More Time

The only person who can motivate you is yourself. Therefore as a leader you cannot motivate the members of your team, your followers. You can, however, create a motivating environment in which your team can flourish. You need to recognise your responsibility as a leader to develop your staff and find ways to encourage them to manifest their potential into actuality. Developing a learning environment needs to be cultivated and considered. A balance needs to be struck between accommodation of failure and supporting the learning process for growth and development. Careful attention to this is recommended to ensure that growth is not stifled.

Coaching is an effective process which supports staff development. Delegation is an effective tool through which potential can be actualised. Leaders who have invested time in coaching can be happy in the knowledge that they are manifesting leadership principles in helping others make their contribution to the organisation. This action seeks to reveal your strength as a leader, demonstrating the satisfaction of shared achievements and valuing the contribution of all through goals and projects that embrace both task and people. The latter may be considered the building blocks for relationships and a positive working environment.

Motivation comes from the Latin word 'moveo' – to move. Visualise what this could mean in a working environment. Imagine, for a moment, an organisation with everyone motivated. The output of activity would be significantly increased with all the followers having a greater self-belief. From an organisational context this energy would be infectious, with individuals being more buzzed up with their increasing contributions and a sense of fulfilment in the achievement of organisational goals.

THE CARE OF DEVELOPMENT AND DELEGATION

Consider carefully the below questions and statements and then use the space provided to write down your answers.

Developing Self

- In what ways are you developing yourself as a leader?
- What evidence exists of this development?
- How do your team members respond to you?
- Do you develop all aspects of your life, knowing that as you do you develop holistically?
- What do you need to do in work or outside to remain optimally motivated?
- Are you fearful of letting go control in relation to your role and therefore shun delegation, preferring to be overburdened in order to be seen as carrying a heavy weight of responsibility all by yourself?
- What is the nagging fear inside of you? Can you name it? What do you want to do about this?
- If you answer truthfully, what is the main obstacle preventing you from delegating?

_____

_____

_____

_____

_____

_____

_____

_____

_____

_____

_____

Developing Followers

- Could you consider spending time with one member of your team, coaching them and thereby enriching their role and allowing them contribute at a higher level this month?
- What has stopped you from doing this in the last week? Last month?
- Have you acknowledged the contributions of others? Do you do this consistently?
- Are you specific when you give positive feedback?
- When you give feedback are you consciously aware of the reaction and its effect on your followers?
- Have you overlooked someone because you were too busy and didn't praise them for their efforts?
- What evidence exists to support the supposition that you have created an environment to motivate members of your team?
- As a leader in this organisation have you sought to influence others to create an environment across the organisation which encourages the development of the workforce?
- Have you received feedback or have you requested feedback in relation to your leadership style?

_____

_____

_____

_____

_____

_____

_____

_____

_____

_____

_____

_____

COMMITMENT TO TAKE ACTION

Before completing this final section take the time to review what you have written up to now. Then create a space, some quiet time, for you to really connect with yourself and see what you truly want to commit to.

For this process stay out of your head as much as possible and instead connect with your heart. Ask of it what is best for you at this time to commit to. When you are ready, take up to three actions to work on over the coming months.

Set these as goals in SMART format, ensuring that you are including specific details on the actions necessary. You also will need to measure your progress so decide on the measurement and the frequency for each undertaking. Then transfer these actions and goals to your regular working documents, e.g. your diary.

Finally, before leaving this chapter please sign and date your commitment to these actions below.

Chapter 7 – Development: Goal 1

_____
_____
_____
_____
_____

Chapter 7 – Development: Goal 2

_____
_____
_____
_____
_____

Chapter 7 – Development: Goal 3

_____

_____

_____

_____

_____

Sign and Date

_____   _____

Accountability and Achievement of Aims

Acknowledgement of Actions

'It is wrong and immoral to seek to escape the consequences of one's acts.'

Mahatma Gandhi

Introduction

This chapter presents a variety of themes, starting with accountability. A discussion on achievement of aims/goals follows and develops into the importance of acknowledgement of actions. Acknowledging the contribution of others is integral to this.

Accountability

Ultimately, the buck stops with the leader. Accountability is firmly planted on your shoulders. As the leader, you own the ultimate result – pass or fail. Delegation, an essential activity within the leadership role, does not abdicate you from accountability.

Although delegation has been previously discussed, it is worth a further mention in the context of accountability. For delegation to work effectively agreement has to be reached with all the parties involved. This includes the goal, the scope, expected outcomes and, not least, the monitoring frequency and follow-up. Lack of adequate follow-up on delegated activities may lead to the failure of a project, with the accountability and blame resting solely on you.

The simple rule is: hold power accountable (Gardner, 1993).

Achievement of Aims

Many people dream and have desires of what they would like to be, do or have. Some may go as far as committing these to paper in the form of goals (aims). But lacking actions, these goals go no further; they are mere aspirations. We all have faced a lack of commitment towards the New Year resolutions we make so ardently on 1 January. Personal goals can somehow get sidetracked, receiving lesser attention and focus, while work goals appear to meet with greater commitment and greater completion rates. As human beings we are many parts, playing several roles within our daily lives, so therefore both work and personal goals merit equal attention.

Goals become a reality when action is taken coupled with consistent effort. This can be the stumbling block for many people. Without effort, things are left to chance and we wonder why we become disappointed and disillusioned with life when our goals do not come to fruition. Inaction is actually an action in itself, albeit not a very helpful one if we are in earnest about the goal we have set. So, if we want to get a different result we need to take a different action.

To any stimulus, event or desire we have the ability to respond and take action. The type of action we take is down to the choices we make. These actions affect our goals.

In the context of organisations, goals become a standard way of life, with the setting of departmental, team and individual goals. These goals in turn support the higher-order goals, the organisational objectives which have been set to direct organisational success. Organisational goals need to continually reflect and derive their meaning from the organisation's vision.

The all-important vision is the why – why was the organisation founded? Knowing the why – the purpose, cause or belief – gives the ability to inspire all. The vision, the organisation's purpose for being, drives the organisation to growth and success. Followers and leaders alike need to know the meaning behind their efforts and align to the belief in the vision. Knowing the 'why' is how all great leaders inspire and knowing the 'how' (i.e. the actions to take) is what brings success to organisations. This connects leaders and followers to their purpose.

Achievement of a goal is a wonderful feeling, but how often do you take time out to pause and acknowledge your achievements? Are you caught up in the flow of a hectic lifestyle moving ceaselessly from one goal completion to another goal start cycle?

Acknowledgement or Appreciation

It is beneficial and indeed satisfying to take a welcome pause, draw your breath and acknowledge your efforts or those of another before you move onto yet another activity. This reflective period can be the ground for fertile renewal. It can provide the impetus to do more and achieve more. This pause for acknowledgement can create the separation necessary from an incessant urgency mode, a mode of constant activity. It is in this space that you have the possibility of appreciating your achievements and the journey you have undertaken to get there: appreciating the obstacles you have overcome with determination, strength and resilience to succeed.

We talk of money or investments appreciating in value and becoming greater. You spend considerable portions of your life carefully monitoring these investments and assets to ensure that you get the best possible return, that they appreciate in value. Why not spend time appreciating yourself and others? Acknowledging the efforts of someone or showing appreciation is paramount to your role as a leader.

Appreciation can set us up for much success. So it is good to shift your attention and focus directly on the acknowledgement and appreciation of people. You can spend vast sums of money advertising, interviewing and selecting the right candidate for the right position. You finally hire them and put them through an induction programme, role-specific training and possibly further training, and then follow with the appraisal review cycle. But when all is said and done have you really even appreciated the work done by them? What does it take for you to take action on this critical activity?

Appreciation can come in various forms, but the format that works best is honest and timely feedback. The timeliness of feedback can never be overstated. Looking into the eyes of someone as you genuinely appreciate them is a wonderful gift you can give regularly.

THE CARE OF ACCOUNTABILITY, ACHIEVEMENT OF AIMS, ACKNOWLEDGEMENT AND APPRECIATION OF ACTIONS

Consider carefully the below questions and statements and then use the space provided to write down your answers.

Accountability

- Do you hold yourself ultimately accountable for the actions taken in the achievement of your aims?
- Do you tend to blame others or the team when results are not as optimistic as you expected?
- Do you fail to understand the why of your role in supporting your followers?

_____

_____

_____

_____

_____

_____

_____

_____

_____

_____

_____

_____

Achievement of Aims

- Have you truly taken in the achievements? Have you stopped and paused to acknowledge them? Or are you moving on immediately to the next aim/goal?
- What does ignoring the achievements cost you now? Ultimately?
- Have you stopped to renew your energy?
- What actions are you not taking today which are preventing you from achieving your aims?
- Why do you not support yourself to take the action you need in the achievement of your goals?

- In what ways do you sabotage yourself from taking action?
- What action do you now choose to take to support yourself better?

_____

_____

_____

_____

_____

_____

_____

_____

_____

_____

_____

_____

Acknowledgement and Appreciation of Actions

Self

- What gifts and talents within yourself can you acknowledge and appreciate today? Can you take action and reflect on these?
- Have you taken any time out today to appreciate nature around you?
- Have you taken the time to see the people in your life and look for the gift they bring to your life?

_____

_____

_____

_____

_____

_____

_____

_____

_____

_____

_____

Interaction with Followers

- What actions do you engage in that support your staff?
- What actions do you engage in that negate the effectiveness of the team?
- What do you now choose to do after this reflection?
- When was the last time you appreciated your staff not collectively but individually? What was it that you appreciated? How did you go about to this? What was the reaction?
- Does the act of appreciating someone have to be related with a very significant event?
- What are the small ways in which you can appreciate your followers more regularly?
- Are you willing to make this commitment?

_____

_____

_____

_____

_____

_____

_____

_____

_____

_____

_____

_____

COMMITMENT TO TAKE ACTION

Before completing this final section take the time to review what you have written up to now. Then create a space, some quiet time, for you to really connect with yourself and see what you truly want to commit to.

For this process stay out of your head as much as possible and instead connect with your heart. Ask of it what is best for you at this time to commit to. When you are ready, take up to three actions to work on over the coming months.

Set these as goals in SMART format, ensuring that you are including specific details on the actions necessary. You also will need to measure your progress so decide on the measurement and the frequency for each undertaking. Then transfer these actions and goals to your regular working documents, e.g. your diary.

Finally, before leaving this chapter please sign and date your commitment to these actions below.

Chapter 8 – Accountability: Goal 1

_____

_____

_____

_____

_____

Chapter 8 – Accountability: Goal 2

_____

_____

_____

_____

_____

Chapter 8 – Accountability: Goal 3

_____

_____

_____

_____

_____

Sign and Date

_____   _____

9

ENERGY OF EMERGENCE

ESSENCE AND EGO

'The essence of the Way is detachment.'

Bodhidharma

Introduction

This chapter introduces the energy of vitality. It can be viewed as your energy and enthusiasm displayed in day-to-day activities in the performance of your role, say, leading a team, and the effect it has on engaging your team. This energy comes from within and is a reflection of your connection to source energy. To the degree to which you tap into source energy, your essence is reflected outwardly as your aliveness of being. In a nutshell, connection with source energy is you connecting with the highest aspect of yourself.

Energy of Emergence

'Energy' is a frequently used word in our day-to-day language and carries with it a variety of meanings dependent on whom you are talking to. For me, energy is about the reflection of the vital life force which comes from within and is then reflected outwards. It deals with your connection to source energy, of which everyone is a part. It is, in effect, about your divineness from within.

To reflect energy outwards, it is necessary to engage with it in a real way and this necessitates entering a silent space and sitting with it in a personal way. This process involves a degree of searching at a soul level to find out who you are and what you are about – having a real conversation with yourself. Questions which may arise could include: What is my journey about? Am I living up to my full potential? What makes me happy? Do I connect and engage with activities and people who nurture my soul? Do I know me and am I comfortable in my own skin? Can I accept me in all my forms? Are there aspects of me that are not perfect that I want to do something about – something that I need to invest energy in to make the changes necessary to help me grow and develop? Engaging with yourself in such dialogue and taking steps to bring about a different version of you requires an investment of energy. Can these steps bring you into better alignment with the best possible you at this moment? Are you willing to invest now? Is this where you will feel more peace and harmony within you, rather than have a jarring gap which continues to gnaw away at you?

The process which we have been discussing may be likened to a seed which is planted. It must collect and gather sufficient energy and nutrients within itself to grow and develop before it can emerge from the soil and shine forth into bloom. It needs nourishment and energy before any attempt can be made to push upwards through the soil and emerge. So it is with us and our own energy. The energy and vitality which we display is a representation of our connection with source energy – with the essence of who we truly are. This connection with source energy involves going within. We withdraw from the outer world and spend some time in silence and peace to make this connection with the essence of who we are.

For many this may represent a very alien, totally unfamiliar experience. Perhaps it is something that has never been attempted, something to be avoided at all costs – preferring in its stead the familiar busyness of the outer world, in day-to-day living, demanding full attention always. Perhaps it is viewed as an activity which is more in keeping with religious order types – monks and others. Something certainly not for a modern-day person, living a hectic lifestyle mirrored only by an increasingly demanding role in business. But for those who have made the choice and space to experience this inward journey rich rewards meet them. Moving from the hustle and bustle of everyday life and, for a short period on a regular basis, going within, is the key to this process. It is in the stillness of being, and for a while leaving the day-to-day activities of life and business, that you can truly find your-self. This is a special place where gentleness, acceptance and loving are to be found. It is here where you meet your true Self, a constant for you. It is also here that you can find the solution and the answers to your queries, in these quiet moments.

The more frequently this inward connection happens, the stronger it becomes and this in turn makes you more confident. Your connec-tion at this deeper level allows more expression of your true Self, a facet of source energy. Through this process you develop more into your authentic self. Developing higher levels of confidence as you feel more at peace with yourself and the world around you is as a result of filling up and tapping into this source energy. A quiet yet stronger person emerges. One who can gain a greater acceptance of what is, who is filled with compassion and love for self and others. One who connects with people and the world with a strong sense of essence – filled with purposeful conviction. One who knows oneself, acts from a place of knowing and engages with all in a loving acceptance of all.

The regular connection with source energy continues to strengthen you to know and act from the highest state of possible goodness and allows you to leave others to be who they are. This energy of essence shines through (and is visible to all who see). Operating your daily activities becomes easier, engaging with people is better and more cooperative, and being with yourself is more peaceful and happier. This leads to a more sustainable self.

Finding this more peaceful and happier place can be developed through meditation and staying in the present moment. This is where personal power lives. There is no past and no future except for the 'now'. This is where peace and harmony abides; this is being. Now is the ever present. Now opens you up to peace, harmony and joy. The joy of being is the blissful state and from this state love and compas-sion flow from an endless well.

I am reminded of one of Ireland's greatest songwriters, Jimmy Mac-Carthy, and his song 'The Perfect Present', which beautifully reflects the present moment, loving yourself and being in tune with the wonders of life.

Newness is also a quality of this space. This is the energy of essence and brings aliveness to your life, tapping into your creativity and the spirit of taking on the unworn path and trying out new things. Newness takes on courage to be unconventional. It is at the heart of leadership. It is also coupled with the essence of adventure, seeking out, attempting to look at a situation or event from a totally new perceptive. Newness brings freshness to your life and allows greater opportunities for growth, not only from the individual perceptive but also from the business standpoint.

Yes, even in business today, regardless of the sector and its governing requirements, there is ample room for manoeuvring, if individuals are alert to seeking out newness whilst still maintaining compliance. It is good to open up to the childlike spirit of adventure and embrace newness.

A Side Note on Goals

Goals are set in the present moment and are about the achievement of something in the future. However, your focus needs to be kept on the present. The achievement of goals is focusing on the present moment and activities in the 'now'. Each now step builds on another now so that future steps are lived and acted in a now step.

'Now' keeps the clutter out of your life. Now keeps the anxiety and uncertainty about the future out of the equation. Now also keeps the lamenting and discontent about the past from this formula. Now is your saviour. Now is an accepting of what is as it unfolds. Now enables you to cast aside the mental mantle of suffering in allowing you to wear a lighter, brighter cloak bedecked with jewels of freedom and flexibility and bringing joy. Now leaves behind psychological pain and connection with the past.

From an organisational standpoint, think of the goals and design strategies – paint the vision but always do the groundwork in the now. Success is honest effort in the now. Let your experiences be always guided by conscious presence: working, preparing, planning in the now, and not in driving to future goals without the conscious present.

Essence and Ego

Essence has been a thread running through the previous section. Ego and its relationship to essence will be briefly discussed below.

There are schools of thought that argue that we need to 'let go' as it causes separation, preventing us from embracing spiritual awareness and our essence. This viewpoint can set us up for internal conflict. However, if ego is viewed from an alternative perspective and seen as awareness about ourselves as individuals, it may be more helpful. Our survival on earth depends on this ego function. Gawain (2000, p. 62) states that rather than 'fruitlessly attempting to annihilate our egos' we need to appreciate them instead and she suggests that we 'foster cooperation between ego and spirit'. She argues on the merits of educating our egos: 'opening up to spirit can enhance our lives' and that we can develop 'an aware ego or conscious personality that embraces our spiritual energy and views our human existence within the larger universal perspective' (Gawain, 2000, p. 62).

THE CARE OF ENERGY OF EMERGENCE

Consider carefully the below questions and statements and then use the space provided to write down your answers.

Energy of Emergence

Self

- Have you given yourself the opportunity to find out who you are – the real essence of you?
- Do you begin each day in a semi-robotic mode to find that each day starts and ends with the same old pattern? Is it difficult to distinguish one day from another?
- Have you ever spent time with yourself in silence? Are you fearful of doing so?
- What are the consequences of doing any or some of the above?
- What are the consequences of not doing any or some of the above?

_____

_____

_____

_____

_____

_____

_____

_____

_____

_____

_____

_____

_____

Interaction with Followers

- Have you allowed others to be who they are? Or have you insisted on who they should be?
- Have you really appreciated the individuation of your followers? What evidence could you provide to support this? On reflection,

is there anything you could do differently that might have a more beneficial outcome?

_____

_____

_____

_____

_____

_____

_____

_____

_____

_____

_____

Essence and Ego

Self

- Do you know what mediation is? Are you curious to find out about it?
- Have you made any time today to sit in silence and mediate, even for twenty minutes?
- What have you experienced during your mediation?
- Are there any insights, prompts or actions which you need to follow up on?

_____

_____

_____

_____

_____

_____

_____

_____

_____

_____

Interaction with Followers

- Are you cynical of others who travel on this inward journey?
- What has been the cost of this narrow-mindedness?
- Are you willing to take steps to redress this imbalance?
- Can you commit to taking them now?

_____
_____
_____
_____
_____
_____
_____
_____
_____
_____
_____

Newness

- In what ways have you personally blocked newness from entering your business?
- What can you do on an individual level in your thinking and doing to bring in more newness to your work life?
- What actions can you take to encourage your followers to take newness to heart?

_____
_____
_____
_____
_____
_____
_____
_____
_____
_____
_____

COMMITMENT TO TAKE ACTION

Before completing this final section take the time to review what you have written up to now. Then create a space, some quiet time, for you to really connect with yourself and see what you truly want to commit to.

For this process stay out of your head as much as possible and instead connect with your heart. Ask of it what is best for you at this time to commit to. When you are ready, take up to three actions to work on over the coming months.

Set these as goals in SMART format, ensuring that you are including specific details on the actions necessary. You also will need to measure your progress so decide on the measurement and the frequency for each undertaking. Then transfer these actions and goals to your regular working documents, e.g. your diary.

Finally, before leaving this chapter please sign and date your commitment to these actions below.

Chapter 9 – Energy of Emergence: Goal I

_____
_____
_____
_____
_____

Chapter 9 – Energy of Emergence: Goal 2

_____
_____
_____
_____
_____

Chapter 9 – Energy of Emergence: Goal 3

_____

_____

_____

_____

_____

Sign and Date

_____   _____

10

Leading

Listening, Looking and Learning

'Leadership is not a popularity contest; it's about leaving your ego at the door. The name of the game is to lead without a title.'

Robin S. Sharma

Introduction

Leading and leadership may be viewed as a practice which engages an inside-out approach, with its core based on the principles of personal leadership: taking charge of yourself, your actions and your reactions to the world. Such an approach taps into the true perspective of you – who you are, what you stand for, your value system, your beliefs and how you act and behave. Personal leadership can be described as a movement towards the outer world having firstly examined what is deep within. The pursuit of goals and the process of providing a motivating environment for your followers in the fulfilment of the desired achievement of these goals are central to leadership. Listening and looking for clues from your followers provides you with crucial feedback, giving you the potential for further learning in your role as a leader.

Leading

'Leadership is not magnetic personality that can just as well be a glib tongue. It is not "making friends and influencing people", that is flattery. Leadership is lifting a person's vision to higher sights, the raising of a person's performance to a higher standard, the building of a personality beyond its normal limitations.'

Peter F. Drucker

Leadership and management are two distinctly different activities and both have their rightful place in organisations. However, these activities are not always viewed as separate, at either organisational, team or individual level. Oftentimes these terms become entangled with incorrect assumptions being made: that managers naturally lead, and that when one is appointed to the role of manager leadership is a natural given. Nothing could be further from the truth. Organisations in trouble often turn to criticising systems and processes and fail to look at the effectiveness of the leadership process.

At the core of human beings is a code, the set of values by which we live our lives and engage with the world. The uncovering of an individual's value system may not be an exercise generally undertaken and for many the response when questioned on values can be hazy and unclear, even with the most articulate of people. A wake-up call – the unexpected event of a heart attack, divorce or death of a loved one – can be the required trigger to question the meaningfulness or otherwise of the values held. True values, universal values, are at the core of human beings and are constant. They transcend the individual's values. However, they often may be either cast aside or hidden in preference for the more dominant individualistic, ego-centred values driven by human greed. My belief is that the true values keep gently gnawing at us until we tap into them and consciously question the value system which we are holding as the dominant mode of living. With the dawning that change may be required you have a choice of swopping and adopting more universal values, thereby engaging values more in keeping with an authentic life. With the adoption of these universal values you see yourself as an individual and part of a greater whole:

having a greater understanding of the connectedness of human beings as universal beings.

Organisations too operate with a set of values. These may be articulated or not. They may also be in conflict: what is declared on paper may often be divergent from the manner in which day-to-day business is conducted. So, as a leader it may be beneficial to consider whether there is a strong alignment between your value system, your team and colleagues, and the organisation for which you work. This questioning may lead to surprises, and may lead to changes and adjustments. It may also cause a dilemma at the unfolding of conflicting values. Deciding on and living to a higher set of values brings us into a greater sense of purpose and inner harmony.

Now moving from this inner state and looking at your actions as a leader, it is interesting to view how you act and behave. You may ask are these actions and behaviours consistent with universal values? For instance, take motivation. No one can motivate another person – a leader does not motivate his/her followers. A leader, however, needs to create a motivating environment in which the team, the followers, are given the opportunity to flourish and develop. For this to happen you need to take the time to understand each individual on your team and to understand what the motivational triggers are for each. Opportunities then need to be brought forth where possible to enable the growth of individuals so that they can achieve success: personal, team and organisational.

Delegation has been mentioned in Chapter 7 and can be viewed as being central to effective leadership and the development of followers. Coaching is a mechanism which needs to form an integral part of the delegation process.

Leadership is very much a choice. You need to be self-aware firstly, then socially aware and finally make a conscious decision to lead. Leading is ultimately about leading others in the achievement of the required goals. Leadership is therefore a social process, a social interaction – without followers there can be no leaders. The art of leadership needs you to engage in the listening process, listening both inwardly and outwardly, picking up on cues and acting on them.

Consider the word 'lead' to have four distinct activities at its core:

L: Loving your role as a leader
through
E: Engaging in meaningful ways with each follower, each member of your team
by
A: Acknowledging the unique contribution that each member brings to the team and what the team as a whole does
and continually
D: Developing each member and the team as a whole to contribute to their full potential within their roles

Do these fit your understanding of your role as a leader?

'Leadership is not about a title or a designation. It's about impact, influence and inspiration. Impact involves getting results, influence is about spreading the passion you have for your work, and you have to inspire team-mates and customers.'

Robin S. Sharma

Listening

'Courage is what it takes to stand up and speak; courage is also what it takes to sit down and listen.'

Winston Churchill

So to whom does a leader listen? This is twofold: firstly listen to yourself and then listen to your followers. In the first of these you learn about yourself – who you are. Also in the act of listening to yourself there will be moments of silence in which an inner voice, the voice of conscience, will be available to you. Some may prefer to refer to this as intuition. Regardless of which term is used, these responses are coming from within. This commodity may be taken out of our equation in the commercial environment, preferring in its place logic and reason modalities as being more scientific approaches. But why is intuition down-rated? And what are the losses that have resulted from this suppression? Intuition is the voice of creativity. The voice that is nearer to our true Self.

Trust your intuition. Self-trust is the foundation of greatness. Self-trust comes from listening to your intuition, to your 'still, small voice' within. Men and women begin to become great when they begin to listen to their inner voices and absolutely trust that they are being guided or prompted each step of the way. Living in alignment with your true values is the royal road to self-confidence and self-respect. In fact, almost every human problem can be resolved by returning to values.

Reflective practice is a crucial element at the core of this activity – reflection on your values, beliefs and assumptions. For some these revelations may come as a difficult task in itself, with the unearthing of surprising and maybe somewhat disturbing results. This may be particularly so for those who believe that managerial roles go hand-in-hand with leadership qualities. They may even query 'why else were we appointed to these positions?' Choice is always there to make adjustments if needed and to have the will to alter course and adopt different, more effective behaviours and actions.

Now let us briefly turn to listening to your followers. The quote 'You were born with two ears and one mouth for a reason', attributed to Epictetus, a Greek sage and Stoic philosopher, springs to mind. Effective listening skills are essential in the leadership environment for checking your understanding, diffusing anger and resolving conflict situations to mention just a few reasons. This demonstrates your willingness to seek out feedback on how you and your message are perceived by your followers. Much has been written on this topic and no doubt you are well versed on this crucial skill. I will, however, mention a few points which you may find beneficial:

- We are often concentrating so hard on what the follower has said that sometimes we can miss the importance of the underlying emotional reactions and attitudes. These may be more important than the follower's words.
- It is well to avoid arguing mentally when your follower is speaking. This internal arguing sets up a barrier between you.
- Emotions can be contagious so leave any of your negative emotions, such as fear and anger, behind you when communicating with your

followers. These emotions most definitely prevent you from listening well.

- In the heat of the moment try to recognise the follower's need to vent, to be heard or to get your attention. It is vital to listen to understand the follower's perceptions and assumptions, intentions, values and needs.
- Finally, listen to your followers not only with your eyes, ears and mind, but also with your heart.

Looking

> *'There is nothing like looking, if you want to find something.'*

> J.R.R. Tolkien, *The Hobbit*

Your followers and the wider group of the organisation can be used as mirrors reflecting back powerful messages. The most important thing to remember from this experience of looking is that you are open to seeing the effect your message, your communication, has on people, your followers. Seek and you will find how you influence others.

Learning

> *'It's what you learn after you know it all that counts.'*

> Harry S. Truman

It is comforting to know that most of the capabilities that enable an outstanding leader to lead are learned. Natural talent to lead also plays a part. But to bring forth this talent and find expression it needs exercise to be developed. Motivation is an essential ingredient of learning. Equally important are the opportunities and challenges gained through experience to develop the talents of leadership.

Although outside the scope of this book a brief mention must be made of the subject of transformational learning. This type of learning goes beyond incremental learning into deeper learning that requires you to challenge fundamental assumptions and meaning schema that you have about the world. Chris Argyris (1990), a well-known author on organisational learning, considers learning to be the correction of errors. An error arises when there is a mismatch between an intention and the consequences of an action. Argyris's learning theory is based on the concept of feedback on the connections between intentions, actions and consequences. Any mismatch that arises would lead to an inquiry into these connections with the purpose of correcting the error. Argyris (1990) differentiates learning into three different strands: single-loop learning, double-loop learning and deutero learning. Argyris and Schön (1996) provide definitions for these terms. Single-loop learning is 'instrumental learning that changes strategies of actions or assumptions underlying strategies in ways that leave the values of a theory of action unchanged' (Argyris and Schön, 1996, p. 20). Double-loop learning is 'learning that results in change in the values of theory-in-use as well as in its strategies and assumptions' (Argyris and Schön, 1996, p. 21). These two types of learning rely on a process called organisational inquiry (Argyris and Schön, 1996, p. 11), triggered by the discrepancies between expected and actual results achieved. Deutero-learning is 'learning how to learn' (Argyris and Schön, 1996, p. 29), referred to as a shift in the learning system of the organisation: 'an organisation's learning systems is made out of the structures that channel organisational inquiry and the behavioural world of the organisation, draped over these structures, that facilitates or inhibits organisational inquiry' (Argyris and Schön, 1996, p. 28).

An example of an application of some of Argyris's ideas is the concept of the learning organisation, by Senge (1990), and the promotion of system thinking. In the human resource development (HRD) literature many authors believe that transformational change at the organisational level is unlikely to happen without transformational change at the level of the individual. Without engaging in deep learning through critical reflection people remain trapped in mental models which are dysfunctional for themselves and their organisations.

'To lead people, walk beside them. ... As for the best leaders, the people do not notice their existence. The next best, the people honor and praise. The next, the people fear; and the next, the people hate. ... When the best leader's work is done the people say, "We did it ourselves!"'

Lao-Tzu

THE CARE OF LEADING, LISTENING, LOOKING AND LEARNING

Consider carefully the below questions and statements and then use the space provided to write down your answers.

Leading – Your Role as a Leader

- Are you comfortable in your role as a leader?
- Do you really engage and lead your team?
- Do you really delegate to develop?
- Do you trust yourself and your ability to lead?

_____

_____

_____

_____

_____

_____

_____

_____

_____

_____

_____

_____

Leading – Your Characteristics as a Leader

- How would you rate yourself on a scale of 1–10 in relation to the following characteristics?

  - Awareness
  - Decisiveness
  - Empathy
  - Accountability
  - Confidence
  - Honesty
  - Focus
  - Inspiration

- Ability to learn from experience – openness to learning and seeking feedback

_____
_____
_____
_____
_____
_____
_____
_____
_____
_____
_____
_____

Listening

- What is your inner voice saying to you about your leadership?
- Do you trust this inner voice and are you living in harmony with yourself?
- How do your values stack up with those of the organisation? What values are you living from? How do you embody the values and influence others in relation to these?
- Are you listening to the messages and the communications of others, your followers?

_____
_____
_____
_____
_____
_____
_____
_____
_____
_____
_____
_____

Looking

- Are you looking to see the reactions and effect that your leadership is having on your followers and the wider organisation? What are they telling you?

_____

_____

_____

_____

_____

_____

_____

_____

_____

_____

_____

Learning

- Are you open to learning and the correction of mistakes or do you shun them and pretend that they did not happen?
- How is your attitude to learning transmitted to your followers? Are you creating an environment for learning or are you ruling by fear?
- Have you selected anyone for coaching whom you could develop within your team?
- Do you share your ideas and opinions at meetings? And do you allow others to do so?
- Do you ask for help when it is needed? Do you offer help to others when they are in need?

_____

_____

_____

_____

_____

_____

_____

COMMITMENT TO TAKE ACTION

Before completing this final section of this chapter take time to review what you have written up to now. Then create a space, some quiet time, for you to really connect with yourself and see what you truly want to commit to.

For this process stay out of your head as much as possible and instead connect with your heart. Ask of it what is best for you at this time to commit to. When you are ready, take up to three actions to work on over the coming months.

Set these as goals in SMART format, ensuring that you are including specific details on the actions necessary and also that you can measure these, including the frequency of the undertaking. Then transfer these actions and goals to your regular working documents, e.g. your diary.

Finally, before leaving this chapter please sign and date your commitment to these actions below.

Chapter 10 – Leading: Goal 1

_____

_____

_____

_____

_____

Chapter 10 – Leading: Goal 2

_____

_____

_____

_____

_____

Chapter 10 – Leading: Goal 3

_____

_____

_____

_____

_____

Sign and Date

_____   _____

Part III

Putting It All Together – Synergise

'Leadership is the "most conspicuous manifestation of social effectiveness" and implies that a person's social competence is honed enough to attract a following'

(Link, 1950, p. 7, as cited by Day et al., 2009)

The preceding chapters in Part II have led you to this point. By now you have decided on what you would like to do with the material you have read. By taking focused action in setting personal goals for each of the chapters in PIHSREDAEL you will be on your journey to derive the maximum benefit from this book. As with any goal, consistent focused attention on your actions is needed until you arrive at your desired state. If a particular action is not getting you to the desired goal then you need to be flexible and change your actions until you reach your goal.

As stated previously, my recommendation is that you use the material in Part II, taking one chapter per month in the order presented. Incorporate items and actions prompted which resonate with you into your regular duties. Observe yourself closely over the month. As stated in Part I, the Introduction, at the close of each month it would be beneficial to carve out some time for reflection using the questions and prompts at the end of each chapter and follow through in developing up to a maximum of three goals that you would like to commit to. In addition, it is recommended that these goals are formally captured and tracked. Goals, like anything else, are fruitless unless action is applied. A quarterly review would be beneficial as the next step for tracking your progress.

At year-end it is worthwhile completing a reflective exercise to view your progress over the twelve-month period. This action, coupled with seeking and receiving feedback, can strengthen this review and support your commitment to your continuous development. A decision can then be made on what you might consider bringing forward to work on for the following twelve months.

Let us take a moment to view the chapters in Part II as a whole. These ten chapters could be likened to a necklace with a set of ten pearls. To wear this pearl necklace you need to place it around your neck, fastening the clasp at the back of your neck. If you look at the chapters in Part II, Chapters 1 (Purpose) and 10 (Leading) will be the closest to the clasp in our necklace analogy. These prime themes of Purpose and Leading are pivotal in supporting leadership and as such need to be coupled together in the leadership development process. For purpose without being able or willing to lead is futile. A leader having a purpose without follower engagement with buy-in to the vision and the required follow-through of action can be likened to a lone star shining into the wilderness. It may shine for a while, but without the richness and depth of followers its light flickers then fades, unable to sustain itself and lacking the strength to bring its vision into reality. Leading is critical to changing hearts and minds, by passionately communicating the purpose and vision and instilling a compelling reason for all to support the cause through required actions, thus bringing the vision to fruition. Leadership is, after all, about the social interaction and as stated previously there cannot be a leader if there are no followers.

On the other hand, leading without a purpose is also futile. Anyone going on a journey starts off with some idea of where they want to go. They take up a direction to steer themselves on a route of where they want to go. With some degree of confidence they steer the direction until they reach the end goal or destination. Often times slight adjustments are made along the way to ensure they stay on target; recalculations are made so that a better course can be steered to reach the destination. So, not having a purpose can be frustrating. Energy is expended in embarking on a particular course and not just taking pot luck as to whether it is the right direction or even the right destination. The upshot for groups or teams is that not having direction and purpose can lead to all sorts of difficulties. Bickering on a team may be commonplace, with team members not pulling their weight, leading to demotivation and a lack of morale.

Leading involves followers receiving clear communication of the vision or purpose. Followers need to understand the purpose. It is through identifying with the purpose and committing to it that followers can remain true to the course of action, seeing things through even during the tough times. Purpose and commitment to it provides the impetus to press on to the achievement of success. The remaining eight chapters in Part II are supporting aids to the prime themes of purpose and leading.

As a leader it is particularly important to look at yourself in the leadership process. Are you committed to the purpose for which you signed up? Or, more fundamentally, are you in alignment with this purpose? Paying lip service to the purpose will not work. You need to be wholeheartedly in unison with the purpose, otherwise your followers will see through this – your actions will not be consistent with your talk.

When you have consciously made the decision to lead, it is important that you engage your team. They must accept and see you as their leader for them to follow you and give you permission to lead them. Leadership is a choice. It is hoped that you have taken this choice consciously.

I add a gentle reminder here to make sure that you cover all ten chapters and that reading is not enough: you need to take deliberate and consistent action. Be brave enough to alter and amend course if this is required, so being flexible is extremely beneficial.

The important thing to remember is to stay committed to the process. When setting goals it is good to stretch yourself; some say 50 per cent stretch is best. Monitor how you are doing at regular pre-defined intervals.

Be gentle with yourself throughout this process, for growth can take many forms before incremental improvements can be seen and this includes a step backwards at times before finally moving forward.

I am sending you my every good wish along your journey. I would be delighted to hear from you on how you engaged with the material in this book and how it has influenced you in your leadership role.

Appendix: A Sample of Useful Tools and Techniques for Personal Development

Below is more information about some different tools and techniques you may find useful in your personal development journey.

Journaling

Journaling is a self-improvement tool, an active process which connects with your inner being. It should not be confused with keeping a diary. There are a number of benefits that can be derived from journaling as you are monitoring your own internal processes. The process can also be beneficial for the integration of psychological parts within you which previously have been in conflict. The journaling process can also help in seeing the changing cycles within your life. The journaling process connects into the highest aspect of yourself, the source of your essence, creativity and wisdom.

A simple way to start this practice is to get an ordinary A4 pad. Create a space in your day to write about any event which you have deemed as important. Describe how it affected your emotions, your thoughts and your interactions. Also include any realisations which you have gained.

With practice you will gain more insights into your life, how you handle yourself, and what you could do to change and adopt more enabling behaviours. This process makes you more aware and with this awareness you become more conscious of the choices you make. Journaling is a powerful tool for self-growth.

Visualisation

Visualisation is a fundamental process in goal achievement. Simply put, it is about imagining very clearly what you want to happen, as if it has already happened. It is about creating an inner experience of what it would be like to have your goal realised. The best way to do this is by closing your eyes. In your mind's eye paint a picture of the situation, making it as emotionally rich and filled with sensory detail as possible, imagining your goals as if it were already true.

Appendix

The key steps are as follows:

Step 1   Select a Goal

Example 1: 'I would like to be more open to criticism.'
Example 2: 'I would like to be more flexible in seeking out opportunities to learn.'

Step 2   Construct an Affirmation about the Goal

State the goal in a simple sentence, in the present tense as if it were already true.
Example 1: 'I am open to criticism and I willingly accept other people's opinion of me.'
Example 2: 'I actively seek out opportunities to learn.'

Step 3   Picture Your Goal as if It Were Already True

Picture the goal by either seeing it in your mind's eye or by feeling it.
Example 1: Visualise someone giving you feedback. See yourself being calm and open to this feedback. Have a sense that you are ok receiving this feedback and that your body is relaxed while the other person is communicating with you.
Example 2: Visualise yourself starting up a new project which is challenging. Feel a sense of excitement as you know this will present you with new learning experiences which you value.

Step 4   Let Go of It

This means you don't force it to happen. You just relax and let the creative process within you go to work to produce it. Then go about your daily routine – be sure to follow your intuition and be open to growth and change.

Affirmations

Affirmations work on expanding your beliefs and stimulating your imagination. Affirmations can be developed by using a series of positive present-tense statements about the benefits which are to be derived from your goals. Write out short sentences using the points below for guidance and make the sentences as emotionally rich as possible.

When working on a particular aspect repeat the affirmation at least ten times a day. You can read it out and also recite it. Work with each or several affirmations for a number of days.

The following are points to remember when developing affirmations:

1. Write it in the present tense.
2. Write the sentence with positive language.
3. When writing affirmations be as passionate as possible about it.
4. When doubts and resistance enter your mind, write these on a separate sheet. These can be dealt with later (see item 6 below).
5. Go back to writing the affirmation to complete the process.
6. Now review the sheet containing your resisting thoughts, which are the barriers preventing you getting what you want. Develop an affirmation to address these doubts.
7. Keep working daily over a few days on your affirmations by writing them down about ten times and also saying them aloud with as much passion and conviction as you can.

Example – Responsibility

- I am the author of my life and I create my reality.
- I act from a position of personal power.
- I have the power to change a situation by choosing more life-affirming and enhancing thoughts.

Meditation – Going Within

Meditation is a process of focusing the mind on an object or activity. It is an inward focus of attention, concentrating on a repetitive focus such as breathing or a word or prayer. Continue this for twenty minutes or more until the body and mind begin to quieten down.

In the process of mediation be aware that your mind is active but with consistent practice of a method you can reduce reactivity to your thoughts. Take on the role of observer or witness to your thoughts, feelings and sensations as they arise and allow them to pass. When you become aware that your mind has wandered you can choose to gently bring your mind back to your focus word or phrase or to your breath. It is beneficial to develop an attitude of acceptance towards whatever happens during the process.

Let us work through an example of a centering meditation. The key elements needed for effective meditation are:

- Place yourself in a quiet environment that is free from distraction. Make sure to take the phone off the hook or turn your mobile off.
- Take up a comfortable position that you can maintain easily for twenty minutes.
- Gently close your eyes.

- Choose a phrase, sound or object to focus on:
  - Example phrase: 'I am at peace.'
  - Example sound: 'Om'.
  - Example object: A golden light focused at your heart centre or your breath. If you choose your breath focus on the in breath while breathing in and on the out breath as you exhale.

  Using a phrase, sound or object helps your focus so that distracting thoughts will pass. If you get distracting thoughts, once you become aware of them gently bring your attention back to the focus.
- Continue your focus for twenty minutes or so and when you are ready to come out of the mediation gently open your eyes and come back to the here and now and continue about your day.
- Be as open as you can to whatever the experience brings.
- If you wish, you can journal your thoughts and experiences.

SMART Goals

The acronym of 'SMART' goals has been around for a long time. Many of you have been using this in your work as standard practice in your performance management process. It stands for:

S	=	**S**pecific
M	=	**M**easurable
A	=	**A**chievable (and **A**ction-Based)
R	=	**R**ealistic and **R**elevant
T	=	**T**ime-Bound

Let's take an example.

Goal:	I am going to reduce my weight by 14 pounds over the next four months.
Specific:	Yes, it is very clear as to what needs to be achieved.
Measurable:	Yes, I can stand on a weighing scales at the beginning of the process and measure myself regularly over a period of four months.
	Start Date: 01 May 2016
	End Date: 31 August 2016
	I can also weigh myself every week to monitor my performance.
Achievable:	Yes, 3.5 pounds a month is manageable.
and	
Action-Based:	I could schedule in a walk and aerobic exercise every week. I could also decide to stop snacking between meals. I could have an apple as a snack instead of chocolate. I could cut down on eating chips and cakes: instead of eating these several days per week I could limit these to once per week.

Realistic (and Relevant):	Yes, the weight loss is sensible given the time period.
	Yes, the exercise and dieting selected are also sensible.
	Yes, it is relevant as my doctor has told me that I need to reduce my blood pressure and cholesterol levels.
Time-Bound:	Yes, I have stated that I will commit to four months to reduce my weight by 14 pounds.
	Yes, I can schedule a walk of 30 minutes three times per week.
	Yes, I will only permit myself to eat cake and chips once per week.

Reflective Exercise

Reflective practices have been emphasised throughout the book. The benefits from reflective practices are that you can become consciously aware of your behaviours and reactions to a given situation. Then having assessed potential courses of action you can choose to change by taking action for more enabling and beneficial behaviours. Taking action is a necessary key output of the reflective process.

There are many reflective practice methods from which to choose. For instance Borton's (1970) framework has three questions to it: What? So what? Now what?

Let us work through how this can be used.

Question 1   What?

This first question could be used as follows:

- What has happened here?
- What did I do or not do?
- What is my role in this situation?

Example: I got annoyed with Joan (one of my team members) when she told me she needed to go home early and the report which I was waiting on today would not be completed until lunchtime tomorrow.

Question 2   So What?

This second question could be used as follows:

- What have I learned about this situation?
- How do I feel about the situation?

Appendix

Example: I felt very embarrassed for my over-the-top emotional response. It caused ill feeling between Joan and myself. I was still caught up mentally with the issue I had with Frank (my manager) earlier in the day.

Question 3   Now What?

This third question could be used as follows:

- Now what can I do to resolve this situation?
- Now what can I change or do differently that will improve matters? Or prevent a reoccurrence?

Example: I need to aplogise to Joan immediately. I need to let her know that I over-reacted and that I'm sorry. I also need to let her know that receiving the report by lunchtime tomorrow would be quite acceptable.

I need to remember that issues need to be separated out. If I am upset about something, like the issue with Frank, I need to address it early and not let it boil over into another unconnected meeting. A few deep breaths would not have gone amiss after the first meeting earlier in the day.

This is a very simple reflective model. Jasper (2003, p. 99) endorses its use by novice practitioners and students and states that it allows novices to reflect on the 'real world of practice', therefore allowing novices to be analytical of their developing practice.

References

Alderfer, C.P. (1969) 'An Empirical Test of a New Theory of Human Needs', *Organizational Behavior and Human Performance*, 4: 142–175.

Argyris, C. (1990) *Overcoming Organisational Defences: Facilitating Organisational Learning*, Boston, MA: Allyn and Bacon.

Argyris, C. (1999) *On Organisational Learning*, Malden: MA: Blackwell Business.

Argyris, C. and Schön, D.A. (1996) *Organisational Learning II: Theory, Method and Practice*, Reading, MA: Addison-Wesley.

Baumeister, R.F. (1995) 'Self and Identity: An Introduction' in A. Tesser (ed.), *Advanced Social Psychology*, 51–98, Boston, MA: McGraw Hill.

Benson, H. and Stuart, E.M. (1993) *The Wellness Book: The Comprehensive Guide to Maintaining Health and Treating Stress-Related Illness*, New York, NY: Simon & Schuster.

Borton, T. (1970) *Reach, Teach and Touch*, London: McGraw Hill.

Bosma, H.A. and Kunnen, E.S. (2001) 'Determinants and Mechanisms in Identity Development: A Review and Synthesis', *Developmental Review*, 21(1): 39–66.

Bronfenbrenner, U. (1979) *The Ecology of Human Development: Experiments by Nature and Design*, Cambridge, MA: Harvard University Press.

Covey, S.R., Merrill, A.R. and Merrill, R.R. (1994) *First Things First: Coping with the Ever-Increasing Demands of the Workplace*, London: Simon & Schuster.

Day, D.V. (2001) 'Leadership Development: A Review in Context', *Leadership Quarterly*, 11: 581–613.

Day, D., Harrison, M. and Halpin, S. (2009) *An Integrative Approach to Leader Development: Connecting Adult Development, Identity and Expertise*, New York, NY: Psychological Press.

Day, D.V. and Lance, C.E. (2004) 'Understanding the Development of Leadership Complexity through Latent Growth Modeling', in D.V. Day, S.J. Zaccaro and S.M. Halpin (eds), *Leader Development for Transforming Organizations: Growing Leaders for Tomorrow*, s41–69, Mahwah, NJ: Erlbaum.

DeRue, D.S., Sitkin, S.B. and Podolny, J.M. (2011) 'From the Guest Editors: Teaching Leadership—Issues and Insights', *Academy of Management Learning & Education*, 10(3): 369–372.

Fournies, F.F. (2000) *Coaching for Improved Work Performance*, New York, NY: McGraw Hill.

References

Fredrickson, B.L. (2001) 'The Role of Positive Emotions in Positive Psychology: The Broaden-and-Build Theory of Positive Emotions', *American Psychologist*, 56: 218–226.

Fredrickson, B. (2003) 'The Value of Positive Emotions', *American Scientist*, 91: 330–335.

Gardner, D.G. and Cummings, L.L. (1988) 'Activation Theory and Task Design: Review and Reconceptualization', *Research in Organizational Behavior*, 10: 81–122.

Gardner, J.W. (1993) *On Leadership*, New York, NY: The Free Press.

Gawain, S. (2000) *The Path of Transformation: How Healing Ourselves Can Change the World*, revised edition, Novato, CA: Nataraj Publishing.

Goffman, E. (1959) *The Presentation of Self in Everyday Life*, Garden City, NY: Doubleday.

Goleman, D. (1998) *Working with Emotional Intelligence*, London: Bloomsbury.

Goleman, D., Boyatzis, R.E. and McKee, A. (2002) *The New Leaders: Transforming the Art of Leadership into the Science of Results*, London: Little Brown.

Hackman, J.R. and Oldham, G.R. (1976) 'Motivation through the Design of Work: Test of a Theory', *Organizational Behavior and Human Performance*, 16: 250–279.

Herzberg, F. (1966) *Work and the Nature of Man*, Cleveland, OH: World Publishing.

Hiller, N.J. (2005) 'Understanding Leadership Beliefs and Leader Self-Identity: Constructs, Correlates and Outcomes', unpublished thesis (PhD), Pennsylvania State University.

IBM Global Business Services (2008) *Unlocking the DNA of the Adaptable Workforce: The Global Human Capital Study 2008*, Somers, NY: IBM Global Services.

Jasper, M. (2003) *Beginning Reflective Practice*, Cheltenham: Nelson Thornes.

Kegan, R. (1982) *The Evolving Self: Problem and Process in Human Development*, Cambridge, MA: Harvard University Press.

Kegan, R. (1994) *In Over Our Heads: The Mental Demands of Modern Life*, Cambridge, MA: Harvard University Press.

Kolb, D.A. (1984) *Experiential Learning: Experience as the Source of Learning and Development*, Englewood Cliffs, NJ: Prentice Hall.

Link, H.C. (1950) 'Social Effectiveness and Leadership', in D.H. Fryer and E.R. Henry (eds), *Handbook of Applied Psychology*, Vol. 1, 3–10, New York, NY: Rinehart.

Loevinger, J. (1976) *Ego Development: Promoting Advanced Ego Development Among Adults*, San Francisco, CA: Jossey-Bass.

Lord, R.G. and Hall, R.J. (2005) 'Identity, Deep Structure and the Development of Leadership Skill', *Leadership Quarterly*, 16: 591–615.

Luthans, F. (2002) 'Positive Organizational Behavior: Developing and Managing Psychological Strengths', *Academy of Management Executive*, 16(1): 57–72.

Luthans, F., Avey, J.B., Avolio, B.J., Norman, S.M. and Combs, G.J. (2006) 'Psychological Capital Development: Toward a Micro-Intervention', *Journal of Organizational Behavior*, 27: 387–393.

Maddi, S.R. and Kobasa, S. (1984) *The Hardy Executive: Health under Stress*, Chicago, IL: Dorsey Professional Books.

Manners, J., Durkin, K. and Nesdale, A. (2004) 'Promoting Advanced Ego Development Among Adults', *Journal of Adult Development*, 11(1): 19–27.

Marcia, J.E. (1966) 'Development and Validation of Ego-Identity Status', *Journal of Personality and Social Psychology*, 3(5): 551–558.

Markus, H.W. and Wurf, E. (1987) 'The Dynamic Self-Concept: A Social Psychological Perspective', *Annual Review of Psychology*, 38: 299–337.

Maslow, A.H. (1943) 'A Theory of Human Motivation', *Psychological Review*, 50: 370–396.

Maslow, A.H. (1969) 'The Farther Reaches of Human Nature', *Journal of Transpersonal Psychology*, 1(1): 1–9.

Mayer, J.D. and Salovey, P. (1997) 'What Is Emotional Intelligence?', in P. Salovey and D. Sluyter (eds), *Emotional Development and Emotional Intelligence: Implications for Educators*, 3–31, New York, NY: Basic Books.

McGarry, A. (2012) 'Implicit Leadership Theories and Leadership Development', unpublished thesis (MSc), University of Limerick.

McGregor, D. (1960) *The Human Side of Enterprise*, New York, NY: McGraw Hill.

Muir, D. and Zheng, W. (2012) 'The Making of a Leader: A Multi-Faceted Model of Leader Identity Development', Paper selected by the Academy of Management for the Best Paper Proceedings, presented at the August 2012 Annual Meeting, Boston, MA.

O'Leonard, K. (2010) *The Corporate Learning Factbook: Statistics, Benchmarks, and Analysis of the U.S. Corporate Training Market*, Oakland, CA: Bersin & Associates.

Rosenberg, M. (1965) *Society and the Adolescent Self-Image*, Princeton, NJ: Princeton University Press.

Schlenker, B. (1980) *Impression Management: The Self-Concept, Social Identity, and Interpersonal Relations*, Monterey, CA: Brooks/Cole.

Schucman, H., Thetford, B. and Wapnick, K. (eds) (2007) *A Course in Miracles*, combined volume, third edition, New York, NY: Foundation for Inner Peace.

Schyns, B., Kiefer, T., Kerschreiter, R. and Tymon, A. (2011) 'Teaching Implicit Leadership Theories to Develop Leaders and Leadership: How and Why It Can Make a Difference', *Academy of Management & Education*, 10(3): 397–408.

Senge, P.M. (1990) *The Fifth Discipline: The Art and Practice of the Learning Organisation*, London: Century Business.

Snyder, C.R. (2000) *Handbook of Hope: Theory, Measures, and Applications*, San Diego, CA: Academic Press.

Snyder, C.R., Irving, L. and Anderson, J. (1991) 'Hope and Health: Measuring the Will and the Ways', in C.R. Snyder and D.R. Forsyth (eds), *Handbook of Social and Clinical Psychology*, 285–305, Elmsford, NY: Pergamon.

References

Strack, R., Caye, J.M., Lassen, S., Bhalla, V., Puckett, J., Espinosa, E., Francoeur, F. and Haen, P. (2010) *Creating People Advantage 2010: Companies Can Adapt Their HR Practices for Volatile Times*, Boston, MA: Boston Consulting Group.

Tajfel, H. (1978) *Differentiation between Social Groups: Studies in the Social Psychology of Intergroup Relations*, London: Academic Press.

Youssef, C.M. and Luthans, F. (2007) 'Positive Organizational Behavior in the Workplace: The Impact of Hope, Optimism, and Resilience', *Journal of Management*, 33(5): 774–800.

Further Reading

Bass, B.M. and Avolio, B.J. (1994) *Improving Organisational Effectiveness through Transformational Leadership*, London: Sage.

Bennis, W. (2003) *On Becoming a Leader*, New York, NY: Basic Books.

Bennis, W., Covey, S., Wheatley, M. and Bogle, J. (2002) *Focus on Leadership: Servant-Leadership for the 21st Century*, New York, NY: Wiley & Sons Inc.

Bolden, R. and Gosling, J. (2006) 'Leadership Competencies: Time to Change the Tune?', *Leadership Quarterly*, 2: 147–163.

Bosco, G. (2004) 'Implicit Theories of "Good Leadership" in the Open-Source Community', unpublished thesis (MA), Technical University of Denmark.

Bryman, A. and Bell, E. (2011) *Business Research Methods*, New York, NY: Oxford University Press.

Covey, S. (1992) *The Seven Habits of Highly Effective People*, London: Simon & Schuster.

Day, D.V. and Harrison, M.M. (2007) 'A Multilevel, Identity-Based Approach to Leadership Development', *Human Resource Management Review*, 17: 360–373.

De Meuse, K.P., Dai, G. and Hallenbeck G.S. (2010) 'Learning Agility: A Construct Whose Time Has Come', *Consulting Psychology Journal: Practice and Research*, 62(2): 119–130.

DeRue, D.S. and Wellman, N. (2009) 'Developing Leaders via Experience: The Role of Developmental Challenge, Learning Orientation, and Feedback Availability', *Journal of Applied Psychology*, 94: 859–875.

Garavan, T.N., Hogan, C. and Cahir-O'Donnell, A. (2003) *Making Training and Development Work: A Best Practice Guide*, Cork: Oak Tree Press.

George, G., Sleeth, R.G. and Siders, M.A. (1999) 'Organising Culture: Leader Roles, Behaviours, and Reinforcement Mechanisms', *Journal of Business and Psychology* 13(4): 545–560.

George, J.M. (2000) 'Emotions and Leadership: The Role of Emotional Intelligence', *Human Relations*, 53(8): 1027–1055.

Giessner, S.R., van Knippenberg, D. and Sleebos, E. (2009) 'License to Fail? How Leader Group Prototypicality Moderates the Effects of Leader Performance on Perceptions of Leadership Effectiveness', *The Leadership Quarterly*, 20(3): 434–451.

Further Reading

House, R.J., Javidan, M., Hanges, P. and Dorfman, P. (2002) 'Understanding Cultures and Implicit Leadership Theories across the Globe: An Introduction to Project GLOBE', *Journal of World Business*, 37: 3–10.

Kempster, S. and Stewart, J. (2010) 'Becoming a Leader: A Co-Produced Auto Ethnographic Exploration of Situated Learning of Leadership Practice', *Management Learning*, 41(2): 205–219.

Kolb, A.Y. and Kolb, D.A. (2005) 'Learning Styles and Learning Spaces: Enhancing Experiential Learning in Higher Education', *Academy of Management and Education*, 4: 193–212.

Komives, S.R., Longerbeam, S.D., Owen, J.E., Mainella, F.C. and Osteen, L. (2006) 'A Leadership Identity Development Model: Applications from a Grounded Theory', *Journal of College Student Development*, 47(4): 401–418.

Komives, S.R., Owen, J.E., Longerbeam, S.D., Mainella, F.C. and Osteen, L. (2005) 'Developing a Leadership Identity: A Grounded Theory', *Journal of College Student Development*, 46(6): 593–611.

Law, K.S. and Wong, C.S. (2004) 'The Construct and Criterion Validity of Emotional Intelligence and Its Potential Utility for Management Studies', *Journal of Applied Psychology*, 89(3): 483–496.

London, M. (2002) *Leadership Development: Paths to Self-Insight and Professional Growth*, Mahwah, NJ: Lawrence Erlbaum Associates.

Lord, R.G. and Maher, K.J. (1993) *Leadership and Information Processing*, London: Routledge.

Marx Hubbard, B. (2012) *Emergence: The Shift from Ego to Essence*, San Francisco, CA: Hampton Roads Publishing Company.

McCall, M.W. (1998) *High Flyers: Developing the Next Generation of Leaders*, Cambridge, MA: Harvard Business School Press.

Mervis, P. (2008) 'Executive Development through Consciousness-Raising Experiences', *Academy of Management Learning and Education*, 7(2): 173–188.

Morgenson, F.P. and Humphrey, S.E. (2006) 'The Work Design Questionnaire (WDQ): Developing and Validating a Comprehensive Measure for Assessing Job Design and the Nature of Work', *Journal of Applied Psychology*, 91(6): 1321–1339.

Petriglieri, G., Wood, J.D. and Petriglieri, J.L. (2011) 'Up Close and Personal: Developing Foundations for Leader Development through Personalization of Management Learning', *Academy of Management Learning and Education*, 10(3): 430–450.

Schyns, B. and Meindl, J.R. (2005) 'An Overview of Implicit Leadership Theories and Their Application in Organisation Practice', in B. Schyns and J.R. Meindl (eds), *Implicit Leadership Theories – Essays and Explorations*, 15–36, the Leadership Horizon Series, Greenwich, CT: Information Age.

Schyns, B. and Schilling, J. (2011) 'Implicit Leadership Theories: Think Leader, Think Effective?', *Journal of Management Inquiry*, 20: 141–150.

Shamir, B. and Eilam, G. (2005) 'What's Your Story? A Life-Stories Approach to Authentic Leadership Development', *Leadership Quarterly*, 16: 395–417.

Sinek, S. (2009) 'How Great Leaders Inspire Action', *TED*, video online, available from: https://www.ted.com/talks/simon_sinek_how_great_leaders_inspire_action, accessed 20 August 2012.

Spitzmuller, M. and Ilies, R. (2010) 'Do They (All) See My True Self? Leader's Relational Authenticity and Followers' Assessments of Transformational Leadership', *European Journal of Work and Organisational Psychology*, 19(3): 304–332.

Spreitzer, G.M., McCall, M.W. and Mahoney, J.D. (1997) 'Early Identification of International Executive Potential', *Journal of Applied Psychology*, 82(1): 6–29.

Tett, R.P. and Fox, K.E. (2005) 'Development and Validation of a Self-Report Measure of Emotional Intelligence as a Multidimensional Trait Domain', *Personality and Social Psychology Bulletin*, 31(X): 1–30.

Thoroughgood, C.N., Hunter, S.T. and Sawyer, K.B. (2011) 'Bad Apples, Bad Barrels, and Broken Followers? An Empirical Examination of Contextual Influences on Follower Perceptions and Reactions to Aversive Leadership', *Journal of Business Ethics*, 100: 647–672.

Wong, C.S and Law, K.S. (2002) 'The Effects of Leader and Follower Emotional Intelligence on Performance and Attitude: An Exploratory Study', *Leadership Quarterly*, 13: 243–274.

'CARE OF' SERIES VISION

Care of Leadership is the first in a unique series of leading-edge, intuitive and practical human development publications. Ann McGarry's vision is to bring the breakthroughs beyond the book itself. Each publication has an exclusive and fully interactive supporting programme which brings your learning to a deeper level, more personal to your individual journey.

So much more than a GREAT read

If you love this book and you are ready to take the next step in deepening your leadership journey, why not join my highly interactive 'Care of Leadership' supporting programmes.

Email: col@mcgarryconsulting.ie

Three programmes have been designed to address specific business needs:

- Care of Leadership – Executive Coaching Programme
- The Care of Leadership – Corporate Facilitator Training
- The Care of Leadership for SMEs

Future publications and supporting training programmes in the *Care of* series will be:

- *Care of the Quality Professional*
- *Care of Woman*
- *Care of Relationships*

To register your interest in or for further details on any of these future *Care of* publications or supporting programmes, please email careofseries@mcgarryconsulting.ie.

Still wondering what is the best next step for you?
Email coach-col@mcgarryconsulting.ie to book in for a FREE 15-minute consultation with Ann McGarry to discuss your specific requirements.

You can reach out to Ann McGarry in the following ways:
Twitter: @CareOfCoach
Linked In: www.linkedin.com/in/annmcgarry/
Email: col@mcgarryconsulting.ie
Post: Care of Leadership Programmes, 'Care of' Centre, 5 Dun A Ri, Kingston, Galway, Ireland H91K29X